To Woman In Love

BARRY LONG, Australian spiritual master, was born in 1926 and lives on the Gold Coast of Queensland. His uncompromising and practical approach to the truth of life, and love between man and woman, has attracted an increasing international audience since he began his public teaching in England in 1982.

TO WOMAN IN LOVE is a book of letters about love, its pain and transcending beauty, written by women in different countries to a man who offers the purity of a divine love beyond personal considerations. Barry Long is acknowledged by the women in their letters to him as a master of love. His replies are intimate, challenging, compassionate love letters to woman, his beloved.

To Woman In Love

A book of letters

Barry Long

BARRY LONG BOOKS

First published in 1994 by Barry Long Books

Barry Long Books are published by The Barry Long Foundation, BCM Box 876, London WC1N 3XX England.
The Foundation is an educational charity registered in the United Kingdom.

British Library Cataloguing-in-Publication Data. A catalogue record for this book is available from The British Library.

Cover and text designed and set by Rene Graphics, Brisbane, Australia.
Printed on acid-free paper and bound in England by Redwood Books of Trowbridge.

ISBN 0 9508050 8 4

CONTENTS

FOREWORD

Barry Long in his life and his teaching is invoking the spirit of woman, the profound divine principle of love each woman really is in her deepest being. The letters in this book are her cry for help, as she struggles to manifest her being in a man-made world, and Barry's loving responses, always supporting and urging her on to be more true. Although each of his replies is addressed to a particular woman in particular circumstances, they are all really addressed to the same place — the great impersonal She behind every woman — and are a testimony to Barry Long's great devotion to her.

You may wonder how a man, albeit a God-realised man and spiritual master, has such a profound knowledge of woman. It is because Barry Long's own spiritual revelation has been intimately connected to his love of woman, his realisation of her as God manifest in existence and his subsequent spiritual union with She. His knowledge of her therefore arises directly from his union with She or love within.

The core of Barry's teaching is his insistence that God is practical and can be realised through man's love of woman and woman's love of man, through their physical love-making and daily service of one another in love and truth as he teaches it. Essential to this is that woman must realise the love she is, something she knows intrinsically but has forgotten, long having been corrupted by the lack of love in man's world. As she gradually realises the love she is, woman can then help man return to the nobility he is essentially.

This book arose as a response to the need of woman, as I perceived it, while accompanying Barry Long on his teaching tours around the world. As Barry introduced his teaching on love and relationship to many new audiences, I was struck over and over again by just how radical this teaching was and how deeply ingrained was the habit of compromise and selfishness between man and woman. Nobody truly knew what love was any longer: woman was lost in a dream of love which didn't work and made her desperately unhappy, and yet it seemed that this was all there was. Sometimes, overcome by false loyalty to a particular man or a notion of romance, she could not even hear what Barry was saying.

At other times I was deeply moved by the courage of the many women I saw who had heard Barry's message and were dying for love, facing themselves in the mirror of their partnerships, endeavouring to get it right with their men; and also those who had the courage to leave the compromise of an unhappy relationship (often after many years) and bravely face the new with nothing to hold on to but a tenuous sense of something greater that was worth dying for. For these women, alone and often in difficult worldly circumstances, there was really nothing but nature to reflect to them the deeper sense of love and its intelligence which they felt rising within. For these women and all those others who are endeavouring to be true, I trust this book serves to strengthen them in their resolve to be love and to go deeper into that place within.

The letters, from women in all parts of the world, were written over a four year period from 1990 to 1994. The letters have been minimally edited to retain the flavour of the original and the names and places changed to protect the individual. Sometimes the circumstances have been slightly altered to make the letter clearer. Barry's letters have been left largely as he wrote them.

Throughout the book there are references to Barry Long's books and tapes. These are listed at the back with a brief description of each.

And thank you to all the women who gave permission for their letters to be used so that others might gain from their experiences and Barry's replies.

Jade Bell
Editor

A NOTE FROM BARRY LONG

In reading this book of letters from women about their love-lives, and my answers, you're likely to recognise several situations that apply to your life. The letters in the women's own words will be helpful and touching for any woman mature enough to have realised that something is drastically amiss in love between man and woman on this planet. Even so, a moving and sympathetic read is not the purpose of the book. The purpose is to help you, the woman reading it, to find the solution to your love-life — and not just to give you more answers.

Here's the key.

You can have only one real question in your life at any one time. It hides behind several other questions you may think are also yours. But the real one for you now is the one that hits closest to home, probably the one you want most to turn away from. The solution is in that answer. It's up to you to identify the question. Remember, it can't be two questions. You must start with one. Then you must live the answer as you see it's right for you, and not just think or talk about it. The secret is in the doing, the living.

Your intelligence will immediately recognise the right question or right answer. But your fear may not want to face the fact of it. You may avoid it by glossing over it as you've probably been doing for some time. Particularly since the answer will suggest some action. It's easier to read and think than to act.

Don't try to live several answers at once. All experience

in love is similar and it's possible for a woman to relate to several situations. Absorb and enjoy reading the other questions and answers. But live the one that is for you now. Trying to live several answers always fails. You squander the most precious energy, the will, that can change your life for good. And once you've taken the first action, stick to it without looking back. You'll then have more energy to address the other problematical areas, one by one.

Remember, the secret's in the doing, not in the talking or thinking about it.

Barry Long

I am your help,
not your addiction

Dear Barry

I want to tell you about what has happened to me since I started coming to see you. I came to your Teaching Week last year and I have to say that the rug was well and truly pulled out from under my feet by your saying that women in business need to realise that it is a substitute for love. I had a strong reaction to this and have since come to realise that I have put love way down on my list of priorities. Since then love has been working its way up to the top of the list and now I feel there is nothing else worthwhile; that love changes things so much that until I have it, I can't be clear about the rest of my life.

This is a painful state to be in, where all I thought I believed in no longer has meaning. All I worked and strived for now is onerous to undertake. I am not happy in what I am doing. I don't believe in my business and my strongest striving or yearning is for love with a man and happiness. Ambition in the world is a shadow of what it was. And all I want is to sell my business and my house and move south, where I have just spent the last few weeks, and where I would be nearer to my family and close loving friends. But this seems a crazy thing to do as there is little work there and I have children to support.

My yearning is to give up everything I have worked so hard for because it doesn't make me happy. Have I gone mad?

Rachel

Rachel

Coming to my meeting was just the trigger. You already knew that business was not enough for you, that love comes first. You just hadn't realised it. That's what I'm around for — to make you realise what you have already come to know through the pain and joy of living.

The divine life is always like this. Any thing that you put before love or truth will be taken from you — when you are ready to transcend the position you have become entrenched in. And it is painful to the mind and the emotions whose nature it is to hold on to the past. Ever is it thus when the divine moves in an individual.

The task is for you indeed to put love first by opening yourself psychically to the love of man. But you must know from experience that you never again want sex without love. This will give you the strength to hold out for the response from him that delights in being with you, not just in bed but in the other natural pleasures of being together.

If he wants you merely for your body, and not also for your presence, he is not man of love for you.

That being done, having put first thing first, you will have to support yourself and your children. Why not continue for now with your business? It won't and needn't interfere with your opening to man. Ambition is not necessary. Just run the business knowing why you are doing it and enjoy the security and activity it provides.

But I doubt whether the work is the problem. What happened that you are not saying or facing in those weeks down south? Who did you meet? What makes you hanker for down there? Who is it, what is it? Be honest.

'Where I would be nearer to my family?' Perhaps. Perhaps you're attached to them which would mean they're also a substitute for love and will come between you and your love when he arrives. But I don't think so. Where there are 'close loving friends'? This could be it. Does one come to mind? Otherwise 'close loving friends' again can be crutches and substitutes. But I suspect it's someone.

Don't make decisions. Be honest with yourself and the situation by looking at my questions. As soon as you are honest about what has happened to you in terms of some event other than your meeting with me, an energy will be released from your subconscious which will make things clearer for you.

You haven't gone mad. You're going sane. Your life is changing. You are entering a new cycle. But you can't rush it.

❖

Dear Barry

When I discovered your teaching my life was completely revolutionised. I became a new person, blissfully happy as it seemed I had found what I had been looking for. This feeling was reinforced when I came to your seminar. For about two months afterwards, I was on a 'high', living on the strength and tremendous energy that your presence gave me.

However, all that certitude of having found the truth seems to be disappearing now. As you say in your tapes I feel that the world is dragging me down and I am beginning to doubt that it was all real, and not just an illusion. Of course I am looking forward to your next seminar as I am sure that being with you will give me renewed vitality. On the other hand, I am disappointed in my self that I do not seem to have the strength of mind to keep present and aware on my own.

Waiting to be with you is like an addiction. In between times I get withdrawal symptoms when I regress to the old person I was before, confused, unhappy and uncertain. Whereas a few months ago I was brave and adventurous, dying to the moment and being new, I now find I am being pulled back into old habits and choosing to compromise for comfort and security.

I know that I need to live in a spiritually conscious way but keeping on the spiritual path is so much harder and more painful than I had imagined at the beginning when you helped me to see the light.

Do these doubts and barriers always arise after the initial discovery of the truth? If so, how can one preserve that knowledge and defend oneself against the materialistic world?

I am in the process of getting divorced. Discovering you helped me make this decision which I had been putting off for years although I felt I was living a lie. I felt that my husband was using me and that he didn't love me enough. I had hoped that speaking to him about your teaching would help us to make a fresh start together, but unfortunately he was quite hostile. Mostly I am sure that getting divorced is the right thing for me, but at times like now I feel conflict and resistance inside me and become tempted to stay in the marriage even if it is 'second best'.

I would appreciate some advice from you to help me stop going backwards and living in ignorance again.

Stella

Stella

Do not falter. The truth is still as you discovered it — vital and wondrous. It is there in you now, the knowledge, the strength and the courage.

What has happened is this. Truth is an energy for good. It is a working energy. Once it enters, or becomes known in a body, it never ceases transforming the old dark and past emotional energies that previously were dictating the life. These emotions and the habitual thought associated with them are deep and hard. They form stratas of ignorance in the psyche. The truth when it first enters plays in and re-affirms the moist soft ground of love in the individual. But eventually, the energy moves to confront and transform the heavy old resistant stratas. This is what is going on in you. The bliss and joy you knew is now being directed at the past in your being — all those yesterdays of compromising.

These must be informed and transformed for you to be pure — for the truth is the energy of purity. The barriers and doubts are simply the reactions, the fearful retaliations of the resistant past emotions. They don't want to be converted into love by this strange energy; they can't believe it. They feel threatened — which indeed they are — and at times are exceedingly hostile.

That is not surprising, since you have had the courage to start divorce proceedings because you were not loved enough. There are years of disappointment and unhappiness in those old emotions down in your subconscious and of course they are now right in the spotlight and they don't like it. They like to hide away down there, spoiling the life and forcing the person to accept 'second best' out of their own fears of being exposed for the lie they are. The process is literally the death of these emotions — and that's what you will feel you are going through sometimes.

But know that the truth that you are — the truth that is doing this — merely converts old emotion into love and presence. That's like death to old unhappiness, though, and it doesn't want to die.

You will break through this strata, when the job is done. You will know exceeding joy and bliss again. It won't be that long. It's a messy business — the divorce side and the inevitable sadness it stirs — but it must be done, as you know in truth.

So be of good heart, as much as you are able, knowing that this is the way of the truth. For what would be the good of truth if it left unhappiness in the depths of us to rise again some day? What you are doing now is forever.

I am your help, not your addiction.

❖

Dear Barry

Your tapes and your books burst in upon my life in the last hot weeks of the summer. Your truth, your words, have wrought changes in me and highlighted what I have really felt to be true all along.

Along with your books and tapes came a wonderful man, Anthony, carrying them and sharing with me. It was all totally unexpected — and wonderful. We listened to your tapes on making love and began doing just that, and it was a wonderful 'thank God!' experience.

This brings me to the problem. I live with my two small sons and their father, Peter, comes to visit every day. He comes for meals, sometimes I wash his clothes and we help each other out financially. We're just like a couple in a way, except that we have other relationships. Most of the time this situation is fine and when it isn't I surrender as much as I can without complaint.

Anthony felt that if we were to continue to make love and keep each other straight we should live together and he would become a responsible parent to the children. Peter's reaction to this was I could do what I wanted but the children were going to live with him. I couldn't bear losing my boys so I decided to stay put and just see Anthony when I could.

On the other hand, Anthony, I feel, is pushing me for a decision. Surrender or quit. I don't know what to do. All I do know is that I feel right in Anthony's beautiful company — I feel pure somehow, pure woman and I have never felt so complete before. At times I feel that life is pushing us together to make love on earth and be responsible for it but surely being true doesn't involve adversely affecting other people — ie if I drop everything and welcome Anthony into my house, I either lose my kids or have to fight in court for custody and end up hurting Peter and the children.

Barry, could you shed some light on this muddled situation for me because my emotions are dragging me under again and I seem unable to tell truth from untruth.

Sarah

Sarah

Do nothing. Keep looking at the situation. But do not think about it. Act if you can. But if you can't, do nothing. Just keep looking at the situation.

Do not wonder what you can do. That is thinking and playing self-distressing games. The reality is you can do nothing, and are doing nothing, until you do.

Do this and a solution will be presented to you. You will suddenly see what to do or circumstances will change, making a decision unnecessary. Event-ually, something will happen. Perhaps it already has since you wrote.

Meanwhile, enjoy being with the two men and your children as you are with them. Do not look to make a decision or you'll have to make one. Life is not as you think it is. For instance 'seek and you shall find' does not mean that by seeking you will find the truth. If it did, all the seekers of the world would have found it by now, found the answer. When you seek you seek what you already know — like you are seeking to know which man or course (you already know) to take. The law is that what you seek you get — so people get what they already know or variations of it. So they end up just as confused and thoughtfully anxious as they were before, even though the situation may have changed.

Be true to life. Be simple. Be patient. Wait. Trust in the new, the unknown.

[Nine months later she wrote again.]

Dear Barry

I have been with you now for over a year and so much has changed within me during that time. I have had a wonderful experience making divine love with a conscious man and although at times the relationship seemed incomprehensible we stuck with it for as long as it seemed right.

He moved in with me and my sons two weeks ago and moved out again yesterday. I found that his psychic energy disturbed me too much. I felt that emotions were being lifted up from my darkest depths too fast for me to deal with. We parted in love because there has been little if any attachment between us. We both also know that having experienced the 'Bhagavati' and the 'Bhagavat' that we will both find each other again in another body.*

The problem is that all my friends, relations and ex-boyfriend (father of my boys) think I'm going crazy. They all try to tell me that emotions are natural and normal and that I'm turning into some kind of cold, twisted Barry Long robot! They say that I'm being brainwashed by your tapes and books and that I'm totally blinkered to any other form of experience. Am I being brainwashed by you?

Being called crazy doesn't worry me too much since I've always been the odd one out in groups anyway. I'm an Aquarian who enjoys experiencing and I feel love in me right now from my toes to the top of my head. It's great! If this is craziness then so be it!

Something else that I find a little disturbing at times is that I feel like I'm tripping most of the time. Colours are brighter and I feel withdrawn somehow, numbed to the effects of the world and other people. Changes in the weather affect me deeply, I am immersed in it where I live, it is very beautiful. The sky outside now is grey and turbulent, a little rain, a little sun and a moody-looking sea. It makes my adrenalin flow, as if something is going on that my mind doesn't know about.

Does it sound to you that I'm doing OK? I guess I'm looking for reassurance. The little girl in me has already fallen in love with you but I'm trying not to take any notice.

One more thing. I, like many women, experience increased intensity of emotions just before my period. For three weeks I feel calm, for one week I am often aggressive and violent to my children. Little Al calls that woman the Big Bear. I have explained to him who she is and I now am endeavouring to deal with her. Can you explain this? Do you know what I can do?

Yours faithfully

Sarah

* Bhagavati: God in female form — the divine female principle endeavouring to manifest consciously in every woman. Bhagavat: similarly for man.

Sarah

It sounds to me as though you're going sane. Life as I know it is for me to enjoy my life, not just now and again but for more and more moments until it becomes a continuous state of being in harmony with the nature of the earth. You seem to describe your own state as increasingly approaching this. The ability of others to understand or share in this is purely up to them. They, like you and me, have to do it for themselves. No one can do it for you. And you cannot be brainwashed into it. I would say that to be brainwashed, really, is to be moody, doubtful, resentful, confused, unhappy at any time. As those negative conditions of living are not natural, they have to have been learned or acquired in the past. All you are doing is increasingly giving up that condition, giving your brain a good rinse in the natural truth of life: I have no right to be unhappy.

Woman's consciousness undergoes a shift around her periodic cycle. It disturbs her acquired rationality and certainly the rationality of man whose compartmental or analytical way of looking at things devised the rational world anyway. Woman by nature is not rational. She is more like Lilith, Adam's first wife who never came into existence. She is free feeling, uncompartmentalised, a demon according to man's terminology — for he cannot stand the way her presence destroys or threatens his psychic structures.

At period time, woman's consciousness is split. She is half in existence, half out. She resents the restrictions of man's rationality which he has foisted upon her as her thinking rational mind. In her natural state woman is logical, that is, she puts first thing first, love first. Man in his rationality puts second thing first, something before love. And this is the cause of woman's fury.

Her period is the psychophysical release of her pent up unhappiness. She is neither rational nor logical but something in between. She is disturbed in herself and she disturbs those around her. She withdraws psychically to allow the process to function but by the way of things is pulled out of her need for repose by the events and people around her. It is a strange state between existence and non-existence and woman, to be in the equilibrium of love which she is, must eventually take responsibility for the state so that she is able to withdraw psychically without disharmony to herself.

❖

You are never too young to love the truth or God

❖

Barry

You may or may not remember me from the weekend seminar, I am the 18 year old who spoke with you individually.

I have also enclosed a letter which I wrote during the week after your evening talks. I never got round to giving it to you but I still feel I would like you to read it.

I am writing to tell you about the wonder of life and how the Law has worked and is working for the good of love, for me to realise my love.*

When I spoke with you I told you how I felt ready to leave the home I was brought up in and move away. I also said I knew what I wanted. When you asked me what that was, I said, a man who will love me rightly. Both new accommodation and man entered my life just two days after I spoke with you. He is a good man, he has been with your teaching for several years. It feels good when I'm with him. I want to be with him and he feels the same.

I feel incredibly easy and right in this situation and in this house.

Thank you Life and thank you Barry.

Love

Lucy

* Law: Law of life, the reality and integrity behind the order of all things.

[Her enclosed letter follows.]

Barry

I feel moved to write to you about what I am experiencing. Everything has slowed down, including me. During the walk I've just been on (I live in the country), I began naturally pulling back from all my senses. Even though my body was walking, I wasn't. I was in peace within my body. I remembered you talking about the difference between matter and flesh, I was now experiencing the difference. I, the flesh, was just as seemingly big as the matter of the body and the external world. I experienced my body as matter being merged with the world, even the air was matter, and I the flesh within it.

I attended all the talks last week. On Thursday I felt and saw and was the void within me, behind the senses. Finally, all you have ever said penetrated me to the core. I am crying as I write this, but they are good tears!

The void was the biggest thing I have experienced, although momentarily. With that knowledge and authority I discovered an exercise to bring me back into the flesh: as I look without myself I can see within, into the blackness, seeing within I instantly feel the sensation within my body.

It sounds strange talking or writing about this, an hour ago my mind had nearly convinced me to pack it in, how I was failing and too young anyway to understand the truth fully. It really is a cunning devil!

Thank you Barry for being the mirror of my love.

Love

Lucy

Lucy

Of course I remember you — in the flesh. Again you write to me with deep self knowledge, surprising in a woman of your few experiential years. What has to happen now is that you will have to live all that you know as your considerable self knowledge. It has to be realised in the reflection of your circumstances. That is why you have left home — and have now met a man. There is nothing like the interaction between man and woman to test, confirm or shake the reality of one's self knowledge. Whatever happens — the wondrous and the not so wondrous — know that everything passes, moves on. Love, but don't become attached. Do not allow the pressures of emotion or relationship to separate you from the void you know so well. In a way, you have just been born into the world, as 18 years ago you were born into the senses, the earth. As every body/baby comes out of the void and soon forgets it, so is the risk for you in your new birth into the world of man.

[Five months later she wrote again.]

Barry

I seem to have discovered something in me. When it comes on me it is like a thin, subtle veil covering my vision. A sense of separateness between me and my surroundings occurs. I have watched this and the stiller I become there seems more separateness, vagueness and clouding of sight and sound. Then follows tiredness, heaviness of my body and occasional nausea in my stomach. It appears to happen at any time but particularly when I go home to visit my family, although it's not always the case.

I've been staying with a couple of friends recently who have also noticed this dulling of life in my face. They both saw that I had it when I was living with my family and then when I moved in with a partner for a short time.

Whilst I was staying with my friends I was doing a lot of dying within. As I really went through it they both noticed a change; more mobility in my face, more apparent joy and life coming out of me. However, the dullness is still there to a degree. I know it is because of the contrast when it goes. So the veil seems to be there, at least slightly, nearly all the time. It becomes worse or more noticeable every now and then, as I described at the beginning of the letter.

The question isn't how to make it go away but rather why is it there? Do you recognise this in your own experience Barry?

I will keep watching without judgement and thought, as much as I can. It's absolutely fascinating.

Also, I would like to add something about thought and image. Lying in bed one morning I discovered an interesting thing. Images were there passing slowly so that I could look at them. A painful event from long ago was just coming up in slow images. The feeling of pain and discomfort was in my body. The image appeared out of the pain, the pain feeling was first and foremost. I stayed with that, even letting go of the word 'pain'. I was the feeling and tears were flowing. It appeared as a beautiful healing process. Perhaps the most important insight being, the feeling comes first, all image and thought comes out of that alone. Thank you Barry.

Lucy

Lucy

The veil you describe is the veil of hurt, the entity of the past that obscures and possesses every body. It starts forming out of the little, largely forgotten, disappointments of childhood and becomes potentially virulent with puberty. The disillusionment of sex, when the unhappy veil of past hurt of another body enters your body while pretending to be love, strengthens it acutely.

You would have felt the veil much worse after you 'moved in with a partner for a short time'. If I recall correctly, that was your first experience of man as a lover. And you dismiss it with a casualness in your letter that shows a subconscious attempt to be rid of it as something not so important. But that, or any other sexual experience with man, is where the veil now comes from. He does not love you in your precious youth — and that hurts. Woman never gets over it — hence the veil in every woman's body — until she is truly loved.

I endeavoured to tell you when I spoke to you (since I saw this coming) to make love only for love. But how could you know, in this experimental loveless society, what love was? You couldn't. But now you know in your own experience what love is not. That's something. Be more discerning and don't be induced into what you don't want.

PS You are right. All thought comes from feeling. Pain produces worry, stressful thoughts. Love produces peace — no thought.

Dear Barry

I am a young woman, 20 years of age, and I have been listening to your tapes and reading your books for about two years. As I have gotten older certain truths have become clear to me as I endeavour to live a truthful existence. I am currently living with a young man and we listen to you together and often speak of what we discover or know to be true.

I am woman and as woman I know I am love. Often there is pain in my love-making. This pain is brought to life when my partner is not loving and present with my body when we begin to make love. I feel a sex drive and anger in him to which I react by constricting myself so that he cannot enter me as woman. If he does enter me, when I am full of the emotion of loneliness and want, I feel almost sick and I close off. The emotion of utter sadness in me after this experience is overwhelming. Sometimes I am able to contain it and bear down on the pain until it dissipates. If I try and be straight with my partner he often becomes angry and frustrated at my emotion. We are unable to be straight about what happens. He tells me I should have 'a good look at myself' or that I 'over-react' or 'I am wasting time and energy crying'. I then find it very hard to keep the emotion out of my presence, so I simply have to get up and leave. This episode infects future love-making because although he denies it, I know in my being that he is still carrying the past.

I love this man and will bear pain to find truth. Please guide me in being straighter and truer. I want to face my attachedness and emotion — I want to be woman of love.

Christine

Christine

I was pleased to receive your letter and I apologise for the delay in replying.

Much will have happened since your wrote. Life is like that. Perhaps you have solved the problem with your boyfriend in one way or another.

Meanwhile here is the truth of the love of woman as I see it. I trust it helps you.

Woman in her love of man is a giver. She wants to give all. But the question is can she give all to a man who does not love her enough? The answer is 'no'. Her psyche will close off or her body (an extension of her psyche) will close up to his physical penetration or register pain. In both cases she will become emotional. She will be confused and start to doubt herself — her own knowledge — as woman of love.

The first way a man demonstrates that he loves enough (for now) is that he listens to her. He hears what she's trying to say without reacting, blustering, accusing or defending himself. But she must not use emotion to communicate. She must speak straight and in the moment tell the man where and how he is not loving her enough in that moment of word and action. If he loves her enough he will see/hear what she means and endeavour to do better. If he doesn't, she will have to face bravely whether she can stay with him — even though she loves him. A man who can't listen can't love.

The difficulty is that woman in our society has learned to love the man first, instead of loving the truth or love first. This is another word for loving God first. I have described precisely above how this is done. Read it over and over. It's not highfalutin'. It's fact in your experience, your life. Do you want a dishonest or half-hearted love? Then you have to be true to what you want; you might say, die for it.

The root of the problem, every problem, is separation from love

Barry

The pressure these days is almost more than I can bear. The emotion in me seems to come up in a continuous stream and equilibrium seems so fleeting. One minute I see the rightness of what I am doing by being with Michael and the next, the relationship seems false — and that I am not being true to myself. I feel in a continual condition of being emotionally manipulated by Michael, yet when I have tried to leave him the pain of my attachment has me flying back. I long to be free and yet I cannot break the thread that ties me. It seems I have never loved one person so deeply; I feel pinned like a butterfly and never have I known such anger or frustration. I am a fool and yet unable to move from this foolishness.

You once told me I get fixated onto men. Well, it seems that it is getting violently, thoroughly and methodically attacked, this fixation. I'll be glad when it's over.

Marie

[She wrote again two weeks later.]

Dear Barry

The help I needed came a few minutes after I last wrote to you. A friend told me about a therapy. I purchased the appropriate book. The result of practising it has proved to be the answer — the help I need. The block that stuck in my body and would not budge is moving.

Marie

PS What do I long for most? I long to be the knowledge without anything in it, without end. The breaks in the glimpses of it are my hell.

Marie

I trust the therapy continues to provide you with relief from the disturbing emotions you spoke of in your first letter.

Finally, no therapy will work. The root of the problem — every problem, every emotion, every thought — is separation from love. The being of love is the only solution.

It is almost cruel for me to write that. For few have tried harder than you to bring this about. The difficulty is that love — living love — is in the flesh, not in the body. It is true the flesh is inside the body, intrinsic to it; but it is not the body. To approach love from outside in the sense of doing something to get a result is to use the thought of the body and this will never do. Union with love is being conscious in the flesh, being living love, and that is done in surrender. Surrender is the giving up of the body/thought drive to effect a result; then I can sink into the pleasure of my own flesh. Remember flesh is pleasure and it is inside the appearance of the body. It is the place of love inside and where love is made. Flesh is still pleasure, always pleasure — when the restless, trying, ever-discontented body/thought is surrendered. Like now. There is only now to surrender in the flesh to. I who am living love begin there. I am no body: I am love in the flesh appearing in space and time as this particular (comes from particle or partial) body.

You can only surrender so far into your own flesh. It's enough while you wait — as long as you continually surrender into it while you go about your ordinary living which includes everything you ever do. You must not try to separate the flesh from the body by doing, by any decision, comparison, analysis, or thought. Those will make more body thoughts, more wilfulness, more projection, more restlessness — and take you out of the flesh. You must surrender those things — for that is all you have to surrender in order to be in the flesh now. The body thinker with its false notions of love and truth only turns inward — surrenders its assumed position over the flesh — when it has suffered enough from trying and doing.

Love — the natural pleasure of the flesh — is now buried profoundly deep in time. All the time that has ever been now covers it. Your body represents all that time. The body is a bomb of time releasing its distracting elementary (elemental) particle projectiles of superficial existence every moment. Since these particles are simply projections of the past they have no reality other than the succession or passage of time appearing as external events in sense. Thus everything changes every moment — and nothing lasts.

The flesh (inner consciousness) behind the body and its projections never changes and always is. It is the original state of consciousness or love of being before time or the mortal physical body began.

So, only when you've had enough of time and its endless frustrations can you cease identifying with its pointless mortal projections and sink into the pleasure and fulfilment of the flesh — which is now, the immortal (consciousness).

I mentioned waiting. Every body is waiting. For every body — or rather, every consciousness — is waiting to be freed of time. But only time lived in the body in time releases one from time. And then only does the release consciously begin when the individual craves for love in the flesh. Unconsciousness craves for love in the flesh of some other body, instead of its own — and so arises sexuality as it is now practised in these present times, these present bodies. True love, or the dawning of real love, longs for love in the flesh of this (your) body — and so hears what I am saying and practises (as I have described above and elsewhere) being love in the flesh, my flesh, here now. The waiting, then, takes the form of waiting with humility and love (one's own love in the flesh) for love in the form and flesh of another body to come and love it in the flesh.

That of course is a description of how everybody sees love — the making of love to each other. But in these material, deeply physical times it is the material, deeply physical bodies that make the love. And that so-called love mostly only makes trouble, frustration or emotion.

Love in the flesh is only made by he who is love in the flesh. All men, in love, are endeavouring to be this man. He is beyond any woman's choosing or choice. He is not found: he finds thee* or she. When he finds thee, there is no mistaking him for another body, another problem, another sexual encounter or attempt. He is love, living love, unpossessed, unpossessable, unwavering, unvarying — forever thine, forever his in the flesh.

The discrimination to recognise him when he comes — the rarest event of all time — and to perceive him amongst all the pretending bodies, is the power that the flesh of all time is now giving to the woman of these times — she who can wait forever in her flesh, if need be, without compromise.

PS You will have noticed that in my reply I went into the great perspective, the cosmic bodies or consciousness of man and woman. This is in the flesh now, as the flesh is in the superficial body. Cosmic consciousness is knowledge, pure knowledge, beyond the flesh, but within the flesh.

The point is that through my teaching, my being, I am bringing the power of pure knowledge into the flesh, especially of woman. For it is woman's time. But this woman, this time, is not here yet. Present woman is still sexually controlled and manipulated by the old man, the old time, the old consciousness that made this world. That man made the world a cruel and emotional hell, especially for woman — his manifested love. He used her as one of his beasts of burden (it being hard work even for him to build such a Godless and loveless place). Nonetheless he awarded her a special place distinguishing her among the other enslaved and exploited creatures of the earth. He made her his beast of sexual pleasure. And to satisfy his craving for immortality he gave her babies, in lieu of love, to carry on his line. And his world of offspring does carry on with the same misplaced immortal fervour — polluting the blessed earth (the latest over-burdened beast of burden), destroying its nature, decimating its creatures and corrupting the human psyche to the constant edge of crisis by making emotion in woman instead of love. Present woman is a shadow of woman. The woman she is quit a long time ago, withdrawing into the flesh. The shadow of woman here now does precisely what he wants: he controls her by keeping her emotional and using her for sex. She is so much in the shadow of man that she's even joining his armies to help kill the creatures of the blessed earth, the children of her own womb.

Nothing can stop the madness of man's world. Only my woman. I am here bringing the spirit of love, She, out of the flesh and back to earth. She will only come for me. She will not come into this world, that is, she will not come for any man who has this, his world, in him. He must die to his world for her, for love. That is the end of the world for him.

What can you do woman, facing the shadow of your reality in the mirror, and in the doubts and fears of your emotions, while feeling within the love and truth that you really are in the flesh?

Listen to my teaching. It is I, man, here making amends for my world and what I have done to you in my ignorance since time began. Do not think, do not try, do not want. Listen. Is what I say the truth?

The new world is not to be woman's world — for any thought of woman is a thought of man. The new world is love's.

* Thee: the tender loving place in every body.

Woman must wait

❖

Oh Barry

How beautiful are your 'Songs of Life'! How powerful is the respect and translucent honesty with which you tell the story of your journey and pay homage to the Bhagavati and the form in which she revealed herself to you.

I received the tape as a gift from the man with whom I have been living for three years and from whom I am now separating.

Your songs and your story reflect the yearning in me — and intensify it. Yearning for that absolute dissolution in love. Yearning for an absolute end to compromise. Yearning to be released into the fullness of myself. I have been consciously engaged in the spiritual process for 17 years. Recently, I have the sense that time is running out. Even though the pressure and restrictions have increased recently, my clarity is masked by exhaustion and feeling stuck and unable to see the way ahead. I am 39.

It was encouraging to hear on your recent 'Tamborine Mountain' tape that self-realisation takes 20-40 years. The fear of missing the point, missing the boat, getting to the end of my life only to realise I have failed sometimes taunts me. My best often seems hopelessly inadequate and the obstacles seem so powerful.

I am grateful to be able to write to you. When I look for a single question — there is none to ask. There are many that arise but they are either answered immediately or I know that I have to wait for the answer to be revealed by the process of my life. This is an essential part of the restriction that I am undergoing and I had not seen this until this moment. The truth is, as it were, being squeezed out of me (or into me!) by this pressure. Withdrawing projected blame and power is central to what I am having to do. Knowing when to ask, who to ask and precisely what to ask seems to be an entire discipline/path in itself for me.

With love and deep gratitude.

Elizabeth

Elizabeth

Be patient. Do not jump into love when you separate from the man. Stand the aloneness. The unexpected, the unknown that you yearn for — your dissolution in love — is coming. But you must wait. You must not try to fill the emptiness with man: you will choose unwisely. Wait. Time is not running out. You won't miss the boat — it just hasn't docked yet.

Your maturity is required. And it is appearing in your realisations as you undergo rightly the restriction currently besetting you. Woman does not mature at 30 or 35. She matures only in choiceless love. Wait.

Dear Barry

I spent a month on the Gold Coast after a Sunday afternoon seminar with you. The month on the Coast was significant for me because I was able mostly to stay with the feeling within.

When I returned home I lost touch with that feeling very quickly, mainly due to a series of difficulties, the worst of which was a broken relationship.

I had begun a relationship with a man I worked with just before I left to go overseas for five months. When I returned home I put any expectations aside (as best I could) and he seemed to be keen to strike up a relationship again. After a very short while he said he didn't want to be involved; a few days later we were close again and then he withdrew again. This happened one more time before we both decided it couldn't go on. On his part he said he didn't feel enough commitment and didn't want to hurt me any more. For myself I felt too emotionally upset and fearful of getting close and then left. He left work at that point and so I decided to go back there.

After having several months off work he has now returned and so we are working together again. I spoke to you about this before and you said I must stop putting my longing on him and leave him free, especially as the situation is not completely hopeless. Neither he nor I is involved with anyone else and there is still a warmth there.

The day after your last seminar I went back to work and it was worse than ever. I was even more self-conscious — though if I could just do what you said then it would be okay between him and me. I don't know how to be myself around him. I tend to either be funny or 'loving', trying to attract his attention or withdraw my energy in order to stop doing that. When I do relax and feel within myself, I am more able to be around him. But at some point the love inside feels more than I can contain, and the longing to express love overwhelms me.

Today I listened to your tape on death and it struck me that there must be a way through this, as there is when someone dies. When someone dies their love is within you. What do I do in this situation where the other person has stopped loving or rather stopped the involvement? What do I do with the love I feel that is specifically to do with him?

I would appreciate any help you can give me. It is not just with this man that I feel like this, though it is more accentuated there. I can feel the love or life within and a tremendous longing to express it or do something with it. A kind of what now? And a wondering if there is love. And then I remember 'Leave it to Me!' There is a frustration though. How do I live in the meantime?*

With love

Clare

* 'Me': the place inside the reader where love, tenderness, joy and beauty are felt. Barry Long takes the people into this place at his seminars and public meetings.

Clare

The point of your letter, as you say, is that the love you long to express is not just for this man, although he currently is the focus. Your proximity in working together does not help you to make the break that is needed in such an unrequiting situation. Yes, when the other stops loving, it is like handling death when someone dies. But his presence makes this almost impossible.

Anyway, to answer your question, you have to feel the feeling of the longing in Me — just as you would if a loved one had died — and not think about what you're longing for. Can you feel it now? You know what it is without thinking about it, so don't allow the brain to think. You know. That's leaving it to Me, to the greater. Thinking about it is leaving Me. And then you will get personal, or your brain will, and throw up pictures of this particular man. That personalising of love by thought creates wanting which then causes the pain of absence.

You want love, Clare, the love of man — not just this man. Leave it to Me. Anyway, the man has a lot of fear in him. He is afraid of love or perhaps the emotion that gets attached to it.

How do you live in the meantime? Feel the feeling in Me. That's slowly changing the situation and solving the problem. You must wait. And when you are not in his presence do not think about him. A tall order, I know. But nothing else works.

❖

Barry

In your last letter to me you said that 'there is no future (to be concerned about) if you be where you are now'. At times I can stay present but still run away through thought and compulsive eating.

I am feeling very confused about my work. Recently I started work as a teacher and resigned after ten days. It was clear to me I did not want to teach in a comprehensive school.

Now I am looking at various other schools offering 'alternative' educational systems. I am even thinking about staying in one that interests me but as it involves living a community life, I am not sure whether I am avoiding being alone. Also I am disturbed that the school's curriculum does not really get to grips with the issue of making love. On my first visit I was aware of dishonesty in this area within the staff and students.

I really don't know what I am going to do. The answer is not to think about it and do nothing within. I am looking, looking and dying.

Can you say anything please?

With love

Claudia

Claudia

Do not be discouraged. Do what you do. Your path is already mapped for you. You are well across the mountain and the coastal plain (contiguous with the sea out of which you originally came and to which you go) is not far ahead.

There you will get a sense of direction. All the uncertainty you have been through these last years has been to break the subconscious old patterns. These are psychic, not rational. So it is said, only God or the Lord knows how much and how long.

Try not to focus on the need to make love while there's no right man there. You are likely to attract a not so right man and repeat the last experience. Be patient, all is well, Claudia, even if for now it is not clear. You are on course. Do not frenzy yourself into doubtful moves. Wake up each morning and do what you do. If you do not know what to do — do nothing. Your body will get up and do what is needed.

This long haul is the changeover to body consciousness — that intelligence which keeps the heart beating. At present you are coming out of body awareness — the inferior human mental condition. Therefore the carnal mind of awareness places misguided emphasis on the need to make love (when the man is not there). It mistakes the body it is aware of for the flesh of the body of the unconscious in which the love you are seeking is made. Give it up. Be still. Cease now, this moment.

❖

Barry

Firstly I would like to ask your advice and guidance about 'Past Life Therapy'. I know what you have to say about therapy in general, but my reading and experience of the past few years have led me to want to investigate this area more deeply.

A few flashes of 'past' lives have shown me there is something in it. For example, during a meditation workshop a recurring figure (oriental, squat, male) was in my belly, thrashing and kicking in rage and frustration. I went to my teacher who asked me to lie down on the floor and began to rhythmically rub the tendons at the tops of my thighs. Gradually I returned to babyhood quite consciously. I wailed and wailed, curling and uncurling my fingers. In the wailing and the curling and uncurling seemed to be the release of the burdens of a lifetime.

When I returned to adult consciousness I knew that I had been onto something important, both in seeing the figure in my belly and also in the regression. But my teacher's subsequent diagnosis and cure never felt accurate: they didn't reach deep enough. I feel that the energy of frustration and rage personified in that internal figure are still in me and, ten years on, I still don't know how to exorcise them.

Also, I have been reading 'Other Lives, Other Selves' by Roger Woolger. He's a Jungian analyst who moved into this field after heavy experiences during a Vipassana meditation retreat. After reading Woolger's book, I'm attending a seminar with him later in the month.

Where I've got to so far is that it's not accurate to describe these experiences as 'past lives', but rather I see these methods as a way of shifting the focus to a level of this body to make conscious and available unconscious emotional energy which is trapped and controlling present events and responses from behind the scenes; a way of entering the multi-dimensionality that I, in fact, am, and releasing energy which is held in bondage or distorted due to a fixation of attention. (It's as though there is no past, there is only now and in this body is contained all time.)

Is this accurate?

What is the truth of this?

Jan

Jan

When are you going to stop chasing rainbows?

While you seek you will not find.

Past life therapy? There you go again. The dominant male intellectual energy is driving you on into more inanities. If you discovered you were Jesus Christ in a previous birth you would be no closer to the truth. You'd just have something else interesting to repeat and write about and think about. A Jungian analyst? They are unoriginal followers and the ones who've come to me have all been in a mess — and soon decamped when faced with reality. Only originality finds God. And originality is not distracted by illusions of the male-dominated brain. Women today are so male-brain dominated they have forgotten what woman is — have forgotten their original being by remembering their unoriginal selves. Thus your mad pursuit of masters, magic and mystery.

Anyway you write well, it seems to me, and underneath the male intellectuality, you do have perceptions of the problem — the male, sexual spook in your belly. That spook writes and talks through you most of the time while the woman in you writhes in neglected isolation.

Multi-dimensionality? Stop creating blockages with silly male-made words. There is only Me. I am as deep as forever. I am now complete in this dimension of sensual being — once the wearied analytical, speculative male-made clever brain is dispensed with as knowing anything worthwhile beyond the date and the time. Energy in bondage? Woman, your only problem is you are not being physically loved by man. How can he love your body when you spend most of your time in your head?

There is no hope, only love. Do not be discouraged. Wait on love.

PS Your observation in parenthesis is accurate. The truth of this is that there is no way of entering Me, the timeless, except by love as I teach it or great suffering. Since only self or ignorance suffers and decamps at the point of emotional (not physical) death, the body is then left in its natural state — love. So love really is the beginning and the end.

❖

Barry

I would ask you please to give more support to woman who is single, waiting for physical love or a loving man. I, woman who am in the process of purifying myself (not pure yet but endeavouring to be more pure) have to be without man, have to be waiting for him. I might have to wait forever as you, Guru, told me when I met you some years ago, and you were right. And I must not get worried or troubled by this.

But when I hear you speak in the meetings saying things like woman should be loved or she will dry up or get brittle, or that a loving man is already in my life but is passing me by because I am not open enough, it can make me unhappy or doubt myself. I can do nothing positive to bring a loving man to me and I should rest in this passivity, not be told anything that might make me restless.

I realise that you are speaking the truth. But in this purifying process that I am in; letting the sex die in me, starving the need and the desire, killing the thinking and the dreaming and the imagination, I would be helped if you emphasised the still in me, the un-desiring, the passively waiting, the untroubled, the part of me that knows I already am love. And even if no man would ever come to me again, I would still be love and I am loved by God, my body is loved by God as long as it exists — for if it weren't it wouldn't be there.

You who are the noble man, giving yourself utterly and completely to love, would naturally speak the way you speak, I quite understand. And you are very right to tell me not to close off, not to foster any dream of man or harbour a grudge against man. I am listening to that and I am hearing you.

But it must be God's will when at times a woman needs to go without a man, for long stretches of time if need be.

If there is any dishonesty in me or this letter then may this communication serve to destroy it.

I love you more than I can say.

Julia

Julia

First, you must see the error of your several questions. You are asking the questions of other women in a different time who are not I, Julia. Julia can have only one question concerning Julia's position now. Your confusion is caused by your mind's attempt to apply to your life now my answers to other women. For every woman is she who is I and each has only one question concerning her life at this moment: 'What can I do about this?' And then she must live the answer.

The answer to your question is, you are doing it. What you have said is the truth for you. You are purifying your self by waiting. You are living it and that is the purification process. Don't doubt. You must not doubt what you are doing. Wait. Do not compromise. Wait until you die if necessary, for a man of love to come to you. Love is God. God is in charge of love, is the amazing intelligence of love. Be true to love. Be true to what you know in your own experience to be the truth for you. Sooner or later when this divine one-pointedness of love has purified you of the sexuality you have imbibed and ingested from your past ignorant sexual life, the divine love or lover will come.

To be willing to wait without hardness or frustration until death means that such willing love in you is immortal, is actually beyond death. Such love of love, or God, or man, is the immortalising of your love, your being while alive. If union does not occur in existence then I tell you in death He, whose love is also immortal, will be with you. Love waits forever without any sense of waiting and in that purifies its existential vehicle, its self.

I acknowledge for a woman in your place that your body does not need to be loved by man; that you will not dry up as I have said to other women in a different time; that you are sustained in every respect, physically, psychologically, and in the circumstances of your life, by your one-pointed devotion to the good as you see it, which is to love or God — until death; and to me, the master, who is also man here to purify you, woman, who is my love. All this is the sacrifice of your self, that love demands.

But this is only for now, for as long as it is true now. It must not become a position — a fixed concept or goal.

You must get your life right

Dear Barry Long

I'm not happy with my life really, even though there is some joy and happiness in it. Something feels missing. I don't know what to change — whether to give up everything or is it just necessary to change myself, to meditate and be more aware and listen to your tapes and to continue making love in the new way?

I am lucky to have a partner who shares the same interests, who wants to experiment with the way of love-making you talk about, who meditates and listens to the tapes with me.

Martin and I are both quite 'old', we met late in life and have a son of four. With Martin I experienced something I heard you talk about on the 'Making Love' tapes — the golden-ness. During the first three and a half years of our togetherness I felt a golden glow in and around me and between us and often spoke of my 'golden years'. Last year the glow disappeared, suddenly and totally. I am not sure what exactly caused that to happen. That is, I think I might know but am not sure.

Last year we moved into another town, brought a house and Martin took on a full-time job. All this came together. I was totally against him working full-time, yet ended up agreeing to it in the end, out of fear. We then thought that getting a house close to his place of work would enable us still to be together a lot, as he can come home during lunch. Somehow it doesn't work though. I'd never bought or owned a house before. I find it a burden, endless things have gone wrong with it. Energy and time goes into it that I'd rather spend on other things.

Also, I find no people here I share the same ways with. Does it matter really or does it just matter to me because I am neurotically needy of a certain kind of people? I keep having a longing recently to be close to people interested in the truth you talk about; people who are bringing up children with more joy, love, openness, freedom and honesty. Really I want my son to be with happier people now. I want to be with people that support me on my way to truth.

Could you please say something to me that clarifies to me what obstacles I put in the way of my becoming aware and enlightened and happy?

With love and gratefulness for your words on the tapes I've been listening to.

Justine

Justine

You must sit down with Martin and face the truth of life together. While you, the woman, are deeply unhappy about something, your life together is not going to work, your love-making will suffer and you will gradually drift apart even though you continue to live together. You will try to make the best of things but it won't work.

The 'golden glow' you experienced of your togetherness for three and a half years is an extraordinary, real perception. It represents love and consciousness — a divine presence in your life. There are two possibilities why it disappeared. The first is that Martin stopped loving you as he had loved you. If this is so, he will have to be honest with you about why, and you will have to see if you can eliminate the cause together — without emotions — and start again. Otherwise, you are unhappy because you don't enjoy the place or the house where you have moved to. It started from around then.

It is not logical for anyone to be unhappy in this life. For the logic of life is — as all the natural creatures show us — I live to enjoy my life. But unhappy human beings, who are no longer natural, usually choose the rational, unnatural way, instead of the natural, logical way. They move to a place or into a house because it's a 'good idea', it 'makes sense' because of such and such, like being close to work or because it's cheap. They do not look first at, 'Do I enjoy this place, is it right for me — what does my body say, not my brain?' If the place is not right, if you are not happy, the people won't be right and things will go wrong.

Perhaps you are emotionally needy, perhaps there are other things wrong in you that have to be attended to. But first thing first, that's logic. You are unhappy with where you are living — a good idea that didn't turn out. Even if Martin thinks it's all right, it's not all right. While you are unhappy it will affect the quality of his life and some of it will rub off on your son.

So you will both together have to look at moving — unless any other cause of your unhappiness reveals itself. You must find a location and house that suits you both. You must do this together having both seen that it is right. Any hanging back or grouching co-operation by one party will only perpetuate the unhappiness — and it will follow you. You are together because you love each other — so you must do this, or what has to be done, as one. If you can't, you will sometime in the future be examining whether you can continue to live together. Together my love and I can do anything; divided we fall apart.

Please know that I do not tell anyone what to do. You do what pleases you. You ask for my help and I give it as best I can.

Be true, honest to life — the natural life — and you will be true to yourself and every body.

Dear Barry

I have just listened to your last tape from Tamborine and I sincerely wish to thank you for the whole series I collected. They kept me in touch with you. Moreover, they often seem to touch on subject areas I was working through at the time. This time, what you said about honesty deeply affected me. To be honest with my feelings has been a major concern. My difficulty has been in learning to distinguish between various feelings. The psychic garbage seems to be so indefinable that it just surfaces as depression. How can I burn the wounded emotion of being unloved out of my system?

I know I am not grounded in my body sufficiently and I have actually tried to do something about it. I opened myself to be loved physically by man and approached Mark. In that relationship I learned not to be afraid of my body, but that is all.

What happened was strange though. Just as Mark was getting sky-high with the discovery of the idea of cosmic oneness — the love for all — I could no longer handle it. Not that I didn't believe in the truth of the idea. But in the world of Mark's ideas, I did not perceive love, especially at the moment when he was able to make love with his wife. Deep down I had wanted him to be loving yet it hurt me personally. He wanted to keep up our relationship, but I became so confused, especially when there was no longer the freedom to express love physically for fear of hurting his wife (with whom he was now able to communicate). I suspended the relationship. He believed that both relationships could be retained and that it was the dubiousness of my ego that made me think otherwise. The latter accusation hurts so much, for if I take the honesty of my feelings as a guideline, it's more egoistic to hold on to something that doesn't feel like love.

How can I handle it Barry? I'm in a way so disillusioned. What is all this openness and availability to love all about, if it ends up in disaster, in hurt? Did the relationship do any good? Did it earth me at all?

At present I'm so confused, weighing up the loss of a possibility of being grounded against my level of emotional tolerance. It feels as if I was a lot more whole before. At least I was in touch with the higher power. Now the space has been replaced by emptiness. How can I burn this out, this emotional hurt of not being loved and understood? You mentioned at some earlier stage that I would be alone again. How can I handle it Barry?

Love

Denise

Denise

You must endeavour every day to do only what you feel pleases you. This is not the same as doing what you please. You have spent your life trying to please others — mum and dad, friends, brothers or sisters, society and the hypocritical priest in your own brain called your conscience. This last infernal priest, posing as the good, is simply the sum total of the expectations of the others — most of which inevitably conflict and cause a sense of failure followed by depression.

Having lived that way for so long you are not going to

throw off the pernicious habit of trying to please all those demands without some superwoman work. This work you are in the midst of and it will continue until you are free or until you are dead. It is what life is about.

So increasingly you must do only what pleases you. You've got to where you are now — in having to write to me for help — by pleasing the others. You're stuck with the results of that while you slowly extricate yourself from them by what you've heard me describe and demonstrate as 'getting your life right'. By doing only what pleases you now, every day, and not giving in to the unpleasing expectations of others, you'll be starting fresh. You'll not be accumulating 'bad karma' that has to be fixed tomorrow.

Your feeling of being not loved and understood also stems from the other. You have 'loved' everyone but your own joyous, or what should be joyous, life. So you feel unloved.

I wrote to you before regarding Mark: 'He will leave you sooner or later. . .' He came and you enjoyed it (it pleased you). Now (sooner or later) he goes and you are on your own again. But are you the same? No. You are enlivened by the love you made, even though the man has gone. But now your thinker, your priest, feels disillusioned. More whole before? Rubbish. In touch with the higher power? It was not very high or real if it's departed now. You never go backwards woman.

Your trouble is you have put your own expectations on love. You knew Mark. You knew the situation. You should know by now, if you have heard any truth in what I say, that you cannot trust or believe in or expect anything from anyone. You do not need to if you are responsible for your actions, which means always doing what pleases you.

Be available for love again, now, if that pleases you. It's certainly not pleasing you not being loved. But keep command. Stop expecting. Enjoy the love while it's there. Know it (or he) will go sooner or later (or perhaps, bonus, he won't!). Let Mark go, if that pleases you. Or take him as he comes, if that pleases you. There was no future in it that could be seen; you knew that. And now you are disillusioned. You must not become attached to any man — particularly to your expectations.

Come on, Denise, open yourself to love of man again. Avoid the same 'mistakes'. Enjoy the love. But when he does not please you — leave him. Don't look back. It is the feelings of disillusionment, emptiness, confusion and not being understood that you cannot trust. Trust what pleases you as a feeling. Follow only that — and go for it.

You now also know more about honesty as a result of your love with Mark. That's good, isn't it? Unless you are trying to show yourself how dishonest he is. He was dishonest to start with but he's more honest now, no matter how little. That's good isn't it? You helped him. Your love helped him. Now who is your love and honesty going to help next?

Move on Denise. Keep letting go within. Whatever you hold on to will cause you pain.

PS Doing what you please is a superficial mental/emotional condition where you flit from one thing to another, like filling in time. It is the mother of boredom and emptiness. It starts from 'What will I do next?' or 'What can I do now — now that the last thing I thought of or did is over?'

Doing what pleases you is now, every moment. It is not spasmodic. You should be doing what pleases you in reading this letter. If it is not pleasing you, do not read it. And when you finish the letter, do only what pleases you; and after that, again and again and again. If you think about how unhappy you are you'll be doing as you please — which obviously won't be pleasing. Practise what I've said and you will soon get the idea.

❖

Dear Barry

At your last meeting you talked about not acting on feelings, if I understood you right. But I left the meeting unclear of the boundary between feeling a course of action is right and knowing it is right. I can see myself moving more towards just 'doing what I do' but the general direction within which action happens is still very much based on my feelings.

To give you an example in my life: a few months ago I split up with my partner (the second time within the year) and that was dictated by my feelings although I didn't force a decision or choose the moment. It felt absolutely right to break up and it felt very final. It felt very painful for a short time but much new clarity and calm soon arose in me. To cut a long, involved story short, other events then happened which made me see how I had contributed in a major way to things not working out between us. But I had been so focused on what he was not doing right that I failed to see myself honestly. The realisations of my own self-delusion were painful and I felt remorse at having loved only partially. My feeling was then to contact him, apologise, and ask if we could try again.

In the meantime, he had moved to another part of the country and closed the door on our relationship. But he heard what I had to say, spent time with me and is willing to see if we can work something out.

The point is, I went through an incredible range of strong feelings and a whole chain of actions and reactions arose out of them. Within nine months, I had changed from being sure I didn't want to be with him, to being fairly sure I did, to being positive I didn't, to being positive I did! At the moment I have to be patient and see what evolves but the underlying feeling of wanting to be with him remains.

As my feelings changed, I was aware of my changeability but wondered whether 'the right thing' changes from day to day and moment to moment too. Does God change his mind or is he more constant! Or perhaps he sees the movements as part of the broader picture.

The issue of not being ruled by feelings seems crucial to me and if you could talk more about distinguishing between feelings which should be acted on and feelings which are an emotional reaction, it would be very helpful.

Generally, out of all the chaos in what's happened I feel much that was old and obstructive in me has been burnt away to leave more nothingness. In a few dark moments I wished I'd never embarked on a 'spiritual' life course but as equilibrium returns again I see I have to carry on from here and the weight of me is less.

Thank you for your continuing clarity which helps me to face up to what is necessary in this process.

Theresa

Theresa

Do not be true to your feelings. Be true to the situation. This is the golden rule of my teaching. Your feelings swung like a pendulum for nine months and swung you with them. And you're still not sure what to do. That's because your feelings are unreliable. They are based on likes and dislikes. What you like and dislike changes in varying situations, with different people and according to your disposition at the time. Feelings are personal emotions. Personal emotions are what I call self — and therefore are inevitably selfish and cause pain. When you act from your feelings you are unwittingly trying to get something for yourself out of the situation. And that's not love. That's love of self. The world is in such a mess because people are ruled by their feelings most of the time.

Your alternating feelings, as you discovered, were unreliable. But the knowledge behind them was correct — you knew something was wrong in your partnership, or you would not have had the feelings. Disturbed feelings are a surface indication that something is wrong underneath in the situation, in this case, in your partnership. And this is where being true to the situation arises.

What is the situation of a partnership? Why do man and woman form love associations and live together? The answer is obvious: to enjoy being together. That's the situation — to enjoy each other. As soon as one starts not enjoying being together, one of the two (or both) is not being true to the situation. The intelligent question then for each to address in each other's presence is, 'What am I doing or not doing that has changed the situation and made it unhappy or uncomfortable for you or myself?'

This requires great honesty, steadiness and a love of the truth stronger than the urge to justify or defend one's self, one's personal feelings. If my partner shows me where I have been unloving or selfish, it is surely my desire to endeavour to eliminate this in myself and thus be true to the situation.

But if the man or woman feels hurt and acts from those feelings they will start accusing or blaming the other. Accusations and blaming are a sure sign of selfish feelings at work; as are emotional outbursts. Arguments, and other violent language or actions, quickly follow. All because one (or both) is being true to their feelings and not to the situation.

If one of the partners is not honest enough to accept their share of responsibility for getting the situation right again, but wants to enjoy the material comfort and convenience of the association, the situation is still no longer a true partnership. It will go on causing pain or it will break. Or it will have to be broken by the one who is true to the situation of love between man and woman, even though taking the action may break his or her heart.

Dear Barry

I find it very hard not to look for man but the teaching is that woman is the passive attracting principle. I live in the country on an isolated but beautiful property. I'm waiting.

The other day in a cafe a man asked to sit next to me and another woman. He asked my name and we talked about nature and some of the local beauty places. We looked at each other and I felt, do I know you, or is this him? Later, as he was leaving, he smiled a big open smile and I found myself smiling before I knew I was. It was lovely. I asked him where he was staying, as he is only here for a few months. I want to visit him (as terrifying as that seems to me) but don't know if I should. I can't really be woman if I don't know what to do. I don't know if I'm hanging on to an idea about how a woman behaves. Am I dying for love?

There are lots of men around but not straight man and this could be one. Yet in your 'Journal One' you say, 'He is beyond any woman's choosing or choice. He is not found, he finds thee or she. When he finds thee there is no mistaking him for another body'. And you talk about 'the discrimination to recognise him when he comes (the rarest event of all time) and to perceive him amongst all the pretending bodies'. I don't know if I'll recognise him.*

Barry, do I just trust, stay with Me, and love (man) will come? Do I get what you're saying? I have been getting my life as right as I can now but with this, as you can see, I have movement. Is this a distraction the mind has put for me to fall over? Your clarity would be appreciated.

I don't seem to be as you describe, a magnet. One man has come to talk to me in many years of attending your seminars. I don't even attract the wolves. What am I doing wrong or is the question wrong? I give up but if you could give some insight I can take it.

In love

Jean

* See page 36, a letter also published in Barry Long's Journal

Jean

There are no certainties in life or it would not be life. Do what you are moved to do. Don't go with your feelings. Go with your knowledge.

Do what you want to do but don't do what you feel you want to do. What you feel you want to do has a quality of excitement in it, also fear and doubt; you are afraid that if your feeling's wrong you'll be hurt again but at the same time there is anticipation, a rising of pleasurable expectation. What you want to do is knowledge, not a feeling. It is cool and calm. You know you want to do it. There is detachment, an absence of excitement. If it does not happen it does not matter; there'll be no disappointment. And if it does happen whatever happens will be okay. You will-ingly take your chances (nothing being certain in this life) in the knowledge that you will not complain, blame or feel betrayed or hurt if it does not turn out the way your feelings would want it to. You do it, whatever it is because it is right; because it is what you want to do, even if it doesn't work out to any expectations.

You quote from my Journal. You did not choose the man you referred to. He chose to ask you if he could sit with you. You recognised him. He smiled a big open smile and you found yourself smiling back (as though in recognition). You say you want to visit him (despite your feelings of fear). But you don't know if you should. How will you ever know if you don't do what you want to. He could be him — or he may not be. Why don't you find out?

Why do you say you don't seem to be a magnet? This man came to you.

Don't look for guarantees. Don't look for problems. Inasmuch as you have died for love, you know what you don't want in man. And what have you got to lose that you have not already lost?

Only your fear. It is life to do — and it is wisdom to know what you are doing.

❖

Dear Barry

Please can you help me. I am a married woman with children and for the past nine months I have found myself in love with a married man years older than myself.

I met the man that I am in love with at a dinner party where we sat next to each other. It was the most extraordinary experience of my life. I must explain that up until this time I had an ordinary family life — hard work and not particularly joyful but comfortable. I certainly was not looking for another man. However, from the moment I shook hands with this man I felt the most incredible surge of energy flow through my whole body. For the whole evening I felt like a goddess. Please don't think this is a physical infatuation, because neither I nor this man is particularly attractive physically. I'm talking about some kind of energetic experience.

I have not seen this man since that time. As our daily lives do not cross in any way there is no real way that I can make contact without becoming scheming and underhand, which I will not do, as I will not cheapen what is so beautiful. My life seems to have become alive with something. I see him in everything and after many years of subservience to my family (my own fault) I now feel as if I am reawakening. The problem is that although I have never given my husband any reason to suspect that I am in love with someone else, he somehow senses it. Our lives together are no longer cosy. We've always been very close but it's becoming more and more difficult to make love and our lives seem to be drifting apart. I am beginning to feel acutely aware that I have betrayed my husband. In my heart I feel I am an adulteress but all the time I am torn between loyalty to a husband who has loved me through thick and thin (and with whom I have been very much in love) and, on the other hand, an intense longing for union with the man who has recently awakened my sleeping heart.

Please can you sort out this confusion and put me straight because I will not have this compromise in me, yet am not strong enough in the truth to see the answer myself.

Chrissie

Chrissie

You met the man once nine months ago and have not seen him since. There is a grave danger that you are holding an emotional image of him that is just not true. That is not to deny the reality of the energetic love you felt that night.

What you must do is find out what the reality is now. You must somehow see him and speak with him; not to take the thing any further but simply to find out whether you still feel the same. This does not involve being 'scheming and underhand'. That phrase is actually your way of justifying to yourself why you have not acted to discover the truth. Not finding out is the dishonesty. And it is this that, in the first instance, is undermining your family life. You can arrange an innocent meeting. Should you discover that you do love this man — and just as importantly, subsequently, that he loves you — then you will have to do something about it, one way or the other. The prospect of this also is probably deterring you from taking the obvious action first. What I would really want to ask you, to get to the bottom of this, is what happened, what event took place in your life ten/twelve months ago that made you turn away from your husband: like an illness, something he did or the family did, or the sudden realisation that you were being taken for granted or not loved? I suspect it was some such event that produced this feeling for this man and that you don't want to find out and face the truth.

PS Please know I do not tell you what to do, I simply say it as it is.

[Her reply followed six weeks later.]

Barry Long

Thank you for your letter, you have put me in touch with the truth but the resolution of the one situation has led me to see the crux of the problem with which I now need your help.

Now I find that, yes, I was fortunate enough to have this beautiful experience but it was one of those brief, ephemeral flowerings and what happened was my mind got hold of it and has used it as a fantasy which has covered up the real cause of my unhappiness. The real problem arises from a complete misunderstanding about the truth of love.

I got married very young. At the time I was completely devoted to my husband. Seeing that one of the causes of my parents' marriage breaking up had been my mother's outside interests, I gave up all of my own, for what I took to be the service of love. I kind of nailed myself to the cross of motherhood. Here I have remained. What this other man really reawakened in me was a sense of my own self worth. All of a sudden after so long here was someone, who, to my absolute astonishment, saw through the domestic frump to the real person underneath. I found myself positively blossoming. I cannot think that this was so very wrong — it felt so wonderful — I felt so alive.

I've always equated love with giving up the self but the way I've interpreted this clearly isn't 'it' because I've really just been playing dead. I've just become a doormat. It's dreadful to admit it, but I even avoid friendships now because everybody just takes and I simply haven't enough love inside me to stand the strain. People just leave me exhausted. So can you tell me:

What is love? What is self? How do you surrender to love without becoming a doormat?

If this self has to die, how come I felt more alive and loving when this self was allowed out for a bit?

What is a good mother? Sadly, I increasingly see my children as being such a burden — I thought I'd given them everything but realise what I've mostly given them is unhappiness.

Chrissie

Chrissie

For goodness sake, do what pleases you, do what you enjoy. It is your life to live, no one else's. They all have their lives. It seems to me everyone is trying to live for someone else, live through someone else or is allowing someone else to live through them. And so everyone's unhappy.

What do you want? Do it. Don't complain, don't blame, don't accuse. Just get on with it. Love is being honest. Love is letting go, not holding on. Self is not being honest. Self is not letting go. Self is allowing others to make your life unhappy and believe you're doing good. Self is a good mother who gives her children everything and makes them and herself unhappy.

You didn't allow your self out for a bit. You left your self at home and discovered a bit of your love, your life.

Doormat? Now that you've discovered what love or life is and feels like, you know what you don't want. See that everybody else knows, too. You've been a doormat — don't talk about becoming one.

But is that the truth? Only you know the truth. Well, what's the truth, Chrissie?

❖

Love is letting go

Barry Long

I woke this morning to 'nothing exists'.

Am I mad?

If I talk with or think about another body, I become filled with that other body's state, emotions, illnesses; I reflect them (always believed until now it was my state). This helps me help that body but can destroy my space if I hold on.

Your death tape says we should not hang on to another's consciousness. I'm sorry I hang onto yours but I could do with a few comments on this odd letter.

Holly

Holly

Love is letting go. Letting go is letting go of self — all that self would hold on to. What is real remains.

What changes when you let go — nothing. Nothing is love. But something does change — self. It dies a little more — making more space for nothing.

You say, 'Nothing exists — am I mad?'

Yes. But obviously becoming saner.

[Two weeks later she replied.]

Dear Barry Long

Thank you for your letter. I disagree that love is nothing. Love is everything — all life, all truth, all joy.

I realise now, after your letter, I have been trying to let go of love. My love, the love inside me that I feel when all is good.

Woman is love so how can she let go of it? Man is love with authority. Without knowledge man uses his authority and teaches woman wrongly.

I also realise it is not I that holds on — people hold on to me, and I become caught in the nothingness of myself by their problems, their demands, their needs. In this space the knowledge of me (my love) is lost.

Holly

Holly

Be still. Read what I say instead of jumping to your own conclusions. Whenever you use the words to me 'I disagree' (or 'I agree') it means you have got the wrong end of the stick.

I did not say, let go of love. I said, love is letting go. Do not write to me again until you can receive and absorb the truth of my replies. They are precious.

[Within a few days she replied again.]

Dear Barry Long

I did not say you said 'let go of love'. I said that is what I was doing. I misunderstood about letting go.

Please could you explain the difference between letting go and being a doormat or giving up or just being plain depressed? If I let go how do I stop others doing what they like with me?

Also could you please explain your comments on the words disagree and agree — that if I use them to you I have got the wrong end of the stick. Does this mean I can have no opinions? I know this must sound stupid to you but I am very confused.

Your replies are so precious I do not take them lightly, rather as a great (privalige, prevalige — can't spell this word) privilege.

Thank you Barry Long. All the blessings of this day to you.

Holly

Holly

If someone you love wants to go, cannot stay because they are restless (and therefore neglectful of love of you) let them go. Do you want a love that wants to go? Will that not make you both unhappy if you stay together — no matter what reasons you conjure up to justify it to yourself?

But if the restless or unloving (enough) one goes, do not have them back. Once you let go he or she must start again from the beginning and win you all over again just like the weeks or months before the first honeymoon. You will never be a doormat then, will you? You make a doormat of yourself by compromising with your own sentimentality and others' emotionality. And in answer to your other question, you are only depressed when you are being dishonest to love or yourself.

Yes, you can have no opinions when you speak to me. I speak the truth. You do not agree or disagree with the truth.

You know it. You see it. Or you don't. All arguments are based on opinions. There is no argument in truth.

It is good that you persevered with the spelling of privilege — and got it right third time. This shows that before you weren't sure, or had not realised, the privilege of having my correspondence. I know now that you do. That's not an opinion. As you know, it's the truth.

❖

Woman is love
and to be real she
must be responsible
for love
— unto death

Dear Barry Long

On a deep level I am touched and I recognise the truth — this shows almost as a physical response. But on a mental level, the level at which I write professionally, I am confused by what you say. It seems contradictory:

woman is love;
woman is responsible for love;
woman cannot teach man;
woman has to be mastered by man (who knows what he is doing).

How can I pass on my recognition of the truth when my brain is gnashing? I am not asking you how to write an article. I want to be writing about Barry Long and what he has to say to man and woman. But it is my responsibility as a writer to write in such a way that some deeper understanding comes across to the reader and I feel I need some clarification on a mental level. Is that possible at all? Could you please give me your guidance and advice?

Nina

Nina

Thank you for your letter. I trust that you continue to be in a good place and are staying with Me, as well as with me that is thee inside you.

I do understand your confusion over my statements that seem contradictory and will endeavour here to unite the four points you raise:

- Woman is love.

- Woman is responsible for love.
- Woman cannot teach man.
- Woman has to be mastered by man (who knows what he's doing).

Woman is love and woman is responsible for love.

Woman is love, her nature. Her character is her responsibility. This is to be the custodian of love on earth. In your letter you write, 'It is my responsibility (as a writer) to write in such a way that some deeper understanding comes across to the reader'. You will notice the word responsibility. In this instance, you have identified yourself as a writer, just as I have defined woman as love. And you have used the word responsibility to define the character of a writer, which, in your words is 'to convey some deeper understanding to the reader'. In my parallel of woman and love, you will see that the responsibility of woman as love is to convey the reality of love, her nature.

The key of course is in understanding the meaning behind the words. I define love (or writer) as the nature, and the responsibility in both cases, as the character. A man or woman of character is a man or woman who takes responsibility for being what they are and in the extreme, which is the love or woman that I am involved with, will die for it. If you look at the loose way in which character is referred to in the world, you will still see behind it this element of uncompromising virtue.

So woman is love. And to be real she must be responsible for love — unto death. And who is there to convey it to? None other than man.

Woman cannot teach man.

Now, the third point that woman cannot teach man (about

love). She cannot tell him what to do or what not to do in the way that a teacher tells or instructs. Such an attempt involves projection, which is a male trait and will eventually make her emotional (forcibly projective). This is out of character with love, her nature. So woman is not in character or responsible when she tries to instruct man or bully him emotionally in this way. Being out of character she will not only make herself emotional but will stir defensive emotion or resistance in the man. He will see her as a reflection of himself — and it repels him to see this in woman, his love. All men recoil from women's emotion because it is fundamentally a male projection. And man forever craves his opposite.

Woman has to be mastered by man (who knows what he is doing).

This statement refers to a master of love, such as myself. It is rare indeed for a woman to come into the company of a living master and for him to agree to master her, that is, to take her on. So this point refers to the very few women on earth who are given the opportunity.

The master actually masters her in love. He does this by taking the male sexual projection out of her which expresses itself in her efforts to 'teach' man to love her by being emotional, argumentative, demanding etc. This emotional projection in woman is fundamentally sexual. And sex, as a projection or emotional wanting, is not love.

Sex has been put into woman by sexual man and she is now confused most of the time about what she is and what she's not. The answer of course is that she is love. And for her to realise this and manifest it in the world she must be cleansed of the male sexuality she has come to accept as herself. The master masters her, purifies her by his love and truth. Like a surgeon he removes the female penis, the seething emotion which she has unwittingly acquired. He loves her to return her to the original state of love, virtuous and pure, which God created her as woman — a maiden, a virgin once again, irrespective of all her past experience with men. In other words, he works to return her to her godhead, what once on earth would have been called the state of goddess.

In every man deep down beneath all his sexuality (manifesting as fear of love, greed, selfishness, wanting and trying) there is the pure state of knowledge of God or virtue. But he cannot realise this uninterruptedly while he still indulges in sexual excitement and fantasy, which most men do today. He just feeds his self which becomes his distance from both love and his own virtue. He is then a long long way from home, the timeless place of love or God out of which he came.

To convey love to man, powerful and real enough to remove his selfishness, is the responsibility I speak of as woman's task.

Wherever there is love in woman he will eventually put his sexuality on it and manipulate or undermine it. He does this because he wants to control her, which is a faint echo of the divine impulse in him to master her in love. But to control anything is not mastery. The master does not control. He masters by love and his subject is always free and only submits to his love and truth because she knows it is the love and truth she has always longed for. Man, however, tries to control woman by making her doubt herself, by brute strength, by economic superiority and particularly by addicting her to sexual excitement. He substitutes sexual excitement for the profound passion and presence of love.

So what is the way out? How can man and woman break

the vicious circle?

The only hope for them both at this time on earth is woman, pure woman. So now I give you the fifth point: woman must be in command of love.

Woman must be in command of love.

To be in command of love woman must be purified of her reliance on emotionality as communication. She must be freed of her self, her love of her sentimental and negative emotions. She must be freed of the romantic dream of love she has concocted to compensate for man's lack of love. She must be re-connected enduringly with God, the reality of love and truth on this earth.

Ultimately this can only be done by her being willingly mastered in love by the master. She is then in command of love and no man can ever again manipulate or undermine her. Nonetheless, there are no ideals in existence and being with the master must remain an ideal unless it is an actuality for the woman reading or hearing these words. So what is her alternative?

First, to begin being in command of love woman has to have within her the intrinsic love of God, the unknown. Without this she will invariably confuse love with her personal feelings. God or love is not a personal feeling. Personal feelings, likes and dislikes, change. Love of God or the unknown does not. It's there more or less, all the time.

Second, woman has to know that love is not for her personal pleasure or security. She has to realise that love of man has a purpose. That purpose in the first instance is to bring more love into her self. This will show as a gradual reduction in her emotionality, self-doubt and negative feelings and a slow improvement in her external circumstances.

In the second instance the purpose of love is to bring more love into the world. That is, by her honesty and responsibility for love and truth, to help man abandon the negative emotions obscuring his natural love and beauty. For man and woman are each essentially an expression of divine love and purpose. They are a union now overwhelmed and divided by false notions and beliefs of what love and truth are. To return to what I am as a man or woman is the only purpose of love between them.

Since woman must avoid trying to teach man, what can she do? Like the master, she must know what she is doing in love. If she doesn't know what she's doing she obviously won't be in command. She must come from her pure experience and know what she does not want in love.

Pure experience is like the experience of treading on broken glass with bare feet. It's not a matter of whether the glass was a pretty colour or whether it was your favourite heirloom — those considerations are personal attachments, personal emotions. The reality or pure experience is that treading on broken glass cuts and hurts, irrespective of how beautiful the glass is.

To be true in her love-life she must respond from her pure experience and not only from her 'love' or 'like' of the man.

Since most men are selfish in love and therefore hurtful, she has to look at the fact of her experience of this. Does she want to be hurt again by his dishonesty, his undermining, and sexuality, masquerading as love? She must know what she does not want and not attach any hopes, wishes or personal feelings to the attraction. Remember the attraction itself is pure, as long as she does not put her personal feelings on it. And the way to make the distinction here is to be prepared to die to those feelings for the truth of love. To die for love means she must not be afraid of losing the man because she loves him or likes him. Even if it breaks her heart she must tell him to go when he persists in refusing to be honest to love, to know what he wants most. For what is the good of dishonest love, love that does not really love her, does not really want to be with her, that prefers other things to her?

She must resist being emotional at all costs. If she's emotional she'll lose her clarity and he will dismiss what she says. He will turn the emotion against her and she'll doubt her own knowledge of love. She will then get even more emotional and next day suffer severe depression, self-doubt, guilt or seething anger. To keep in command, to be responsible for love, she must not blame him or accuse him. That will make him want to defend himself or hit back. She must ask him simple questions such as, 'Why are you restless?' and wait for him to tell her, to reply honestly. His honest reply may upset her feelings but she must not give in to these. She must be able to take his honesty since she is asking for it and cannot allow her feelings to get in the way of such love. Or she will ask him, 'Why are you moody?' A man is only moody when he wants something he does not have and since he says he loves her, what is this missing thing he's dwelling on emotionally? He must answer her straight and not prevaricate.

I trust this is of help to you, Nina. Please receive it as a response to your request for clarification.

Your love and gratitude I receive.

❖

Woman must be in command of love

Barry

At a seminar a few months ago I met a man. He was much younger than me. At first we loved being together and wanted to live together. He asked me to 'leave everything' and 'throw yourself on to life'. Which meant giving up my flat, work and my cat and going off to find somewhere to live together. He also wanted to take charge of all the money and even expected me to change my car (so that everything was new, he seemed to imply). I couldn't do all this, although I thought I could at first.

We separated and came together again several times. At the moment we are apart. I don't think he will be back. He said because of the different sizes of the bodies, he could not love me 'all the way'.

In many ways he is a very beautiful young man, very earnest and not afraid of facing himself, and he speaks of love and truth. Barry, I feel I can't be with man for long. I get restless and unloving. I feel I failed with him. I don't trust that I know what I want any more.

I really wanted to ask you about all this at the seminar but I didn't dare. I was afraid he might leave me. Well, he left me anyway. Or I left him after I refused to rent a flat with him.

He'd already approached another woman after we had separated last time, and I felt he would probably leave me as the love-making and the love generally was slipping away. I feel I failed to love man, through fear. How can I know if a man loves me? How can I deal with my restlessness?

Angela

Angela

Any man who suggested you leave everything as he did and hand over control of your money etc, before demonstrating that he loved you for many months and had in fact and truth taken you on, would be immature and unable to sustain a relationship.

He said (after having loved and enjoyed your body) that he could not love you 'all the way'. I'll bet he indicated he loved you 'all the way' before the first time.

Beautiful and earnest he may be. But you made the 'mistake' of believing him when he doesn't even believe himself for long, yet.

You did not fail him. In your natural longing to be loved, you attached yourself to his early promise — believed in him.

What is the solution? What can woman do when all are so desperate for love?

She must not fall in love, must make the man woo her until he demonstrates he truly loves to be with her, before hopping into bed. She'll lose him? Yes, probably, the way things and man are today. But, if she is strong enough from having suffered enough not to believe him but to enjoy him while he is there, she can make love. But she must eschew the craving to think it's going to last. Impossible? It's got to be done sooner or later, one way or the other. Or woman will continue to suffer — which is abhorrent to me who truly loves her.

❖

Barry

Well, once again I couldn't stay with Richard and so here I am back at home because of my lack of honesty. But there is one incident that has left me in some self-doubt and confusion and I am writing to ask for your perception of it.

I commented to Richard that he was a handy man (he was mending something at home). He then turned to me, put his hand on my breast and quipped, 'Yes I am a handy man!' I felt a sinking feeling in my gut and a sense of violation, yet at the same time no sexual energy from the touch. To shorten what followed, Richard felt betrayed that I should consider he violated me. He said he was only being flippant. I accept that there was a connection with past in me in my reaction to the incident and yet is it wrong what I felt, unease?

I do not ask out of anger but out of confusion. In my effort to be honest in that incident I am left wondering, in doubt of what I do and unheard by man — though I have received great love from Richard.

I want so to get it right, Barry, I'm so sick of always, it seems, getting it wrong. And yet if I am wrong I want to be sure of it so that I don't do it again.

Nicole

[A week later she wrote again.]

Barry

I am dying for my love in this way.

I have asked to be heard impersonally. So that even if

my emotions come out, project and get in the way, they will not raise a reaction in the listener. For I know deep inside that until I am heard in this way I cannot, willing though I am, deal with the emotions which have come from not being heard by man.

It is a hard thing I ask for and it will require a great love to do it. And I know too that if the receiver of my request is not willing to do it (because it is not true for him) I shall have to say goodbye to him and forget him, even though his reflection of my love is so deep. It is the only way I can be true to my love in here and in existence.

If man can do this for me I can give him everything I have in here to its eternal depths. Recently I have been able to give him more than I have ever been able to before because of his love. But there remains a final resistance to do with this deep emotion of not being heard impersonally by man, and it makes me dishonest to him and until now, to myself, by always avoiding it.

I know that until I get this right, everything else that is right for now will soon be blighted again.

Nicole

Nicole

What you say about yourself and man in your second letter is the truth. If he loves you he must take you on — emotion and all. If he does not love you — and the indication from what you say is that he doesn't sufficiently — leave him. And never look back.

The man you are talking about, and any man, knows nothing about love. He only thinks he does. Woman alone knows love. She is love. So she must take command of love. She must tell him what love is not, not him assume that he can tell her — which he inevitably and invariably will do. The only thing is, that for her to be in command of love, she must die for love. In the face of his stubborn insistence or arrogance that he knows love, she must leave him, hopefully bringing him to his senses, or to his knees, under the realisation of what love means and is. Man can tell you and teach you many things. But not love. That is your domain, woman.

Now get on with it. Die to your emotions as well as for love.

Now regarding your previous letter in which you mention the hand being put on your breast and your sense of violation, yet at the same time the absence of sexual energy in the touch.

Again it is not what he feels or thinks. It is what you, the woman whose breast was touched, knows. He was not straight. He was only quipping, as he said. But the truth is that in truth and where love is concerned — where a woman subconsciously knows she is not being utterly loved and faced — there is no such thing as a joke, and particularly a joke about love.

You have had this knowledge or anxiety indicating that something was not right in the situation (which you speak about in your last letter) for some time and it was that sense of not being sufficiently loved or faced that apprehended violation. This in spite of the fact that the man demonstrates a love of truth and honesty.

But the point here is love. Honesty alone will not produce love. Nor will truth. Love is love. The facing of that love as woman, and the facing of the violation that has made and continues to make her emotional, creates the being of love as man.

Whether you're woman enough I do not know, for I am not taking you on. But it sounds to me that you are woman enough and therefore you will find somewhere, sometime, man enough. For what I am going to say now is the secret of your love, woman. The only reason you are endeavouring to find a man to love you sufficiently as you rightly describe in your latest letter is so that you can make a man of him. It only appears that you are searching for love for yourself. The joke is that the man who cannot love you, in spite of all, misses the opportunity to be love. Until, that is, another opportunity as woman comes to him. To be or not to be love is indeed then the question for him.

Thus, hidden in the skins she put on when leaving Eden, does the goddess roam the world looking for Adam who can see through her masquerade and love her.

From your letter, it seems that you have both done much good for each other.

❖

Dear Barry

My partner and I were in Sydney for your Teaching Week. I'm writing to you to help myself, I think, hoping that just the act of writing itself will produce an energy that will help me in this distressed place in which I find myself.

When we arrived in Sydney our relationship was in a terrible state. We had stopped living in the same house two weeks previously after a period of about nine weeks of absolute nightmare. The problem on the surface seemed to be that I had stopped feeling any love and was afraid it was gone for good. I worried morning, noon and night about whether we should split up or not. Finally, in the end it was a blessed relief when he moved out and I didn't have to feel that awful worry (the pain of it) any more.

But somehow or other we never did quite split up.

In Sydney I decided to split us up a couple of times but went scurrying back each time, as far as I remember. Just after we got back we started to have some really happy times here and there. There were lots of difficulties too, but here and there I would feel great and see how well we 'fitted and suited'. I suppose in those times I was feeling something akin to love (I'm very wary about using that word). Our relationship was alive again — we were being honest, clearing things as they came up, making love. My feelings were sometimes positive, sometimes negative but we were alive.*

Now something's wrong; we're going downhill. Tom doesn't seem to care about me as much. I think my persistent withdrawals have made him shut down from me. He was really loving in Sydney and for a short time after we got back. But now he's different; colder, less interested. And I've started mind-fucking about whether we should split up or not.

I started cutting off really badly a week ago — I had given him a present and I wrote some really lovely things on an accompanying card. I wasn't sure if I really meant what I had written ('my dearest, darling Tom'). They were words that rose up in me but I was terrified he'd believe that I loved him. I cut off. It's very similar to where I got stuck in that awful nine week nightmare before Sydney.

On Sunday I decided that it was only my self that was in the way for me and that Tom and I would be all right if I confronted my personal demon in the form of my negative feelings etc and didn't see them any longer as personal to Tom. I did pretty well for a few hours. I kept all my negative stuff, my doubts etc to myself and only put out positive energy to Tom. But after a few hours I lost my hold and the doubts crept back in. By the next day it was much worse and my doubts grew and grew until today I've been mind-fucking about us splitting up again. This worrying thought about splitting up or not is the thing that does most damage to Tom and me. Once it gets a grip on me we're finished. Could it be, do you think, that it's my self's biggest weapon?

Tom was totally into your teaching when we got back, but now I can see that the world, work and money and practicalities have gotten hold of him again. The other day when we made love (I had to fight all my negativity to take the first step to make love) he wouldn't talk to me while we were doing it. I drew his attention to this and he got resentful and stopped feeling anything in his penis and stopped making love with me. He said he can't talk while making love and that he has nothing to say a lot of the time.

I feel angry about this. I think it's part of his withdrawal from me because I'm so difficult. I am very difficult, constantly pulling away and mind-fucking. I just wish he would love me enough not to mind. And put up with me and understand and love me; and still I'm thinking about splitting us up.

I still think we really 'fit and suit' each other but I need some help here. I wish I could stop thinking about splitting us up.

Dear Barry please help.

Carolyn

PS Tom and I have been together for eight years.

* Fitting and suiting: fitting — to be sexually compatible; suiting — to be emotionally and mentally compatible.

Carolyn

You are earnest and doing your best which unfortunately is your worst. You must be more responsible for love between man and woman. You must demonstrate what woman is. You must be woman in action. You must take responsibility for this relationship.

Do you really think that a man can love you when you are so demonstrably emotionally unlovable? What's so special about you that you can be mind-fucking and self-doubting and still have the audacity or arrogance to feel at the same time that someone should love you?

You have to start giving to the man. You have to be lovable — even if it kills you. You did it for a few hours you say, and then you gave up falling back into your own self-indulgent, self-pitying, selfish emotions. How dare you?

When he was loving to you after Sydney, how much did you really reach across and acknowledge his loving of you? How often did you say to him, 'It is lovely to have your love as you are giving it to me and your recognition of me as woman. I love you for it and I will do all I can to keep my negativity from coming between us'? Did you say this and all the other things that should have been in you at this time to acknowledge his love, every half hour? That's how hard you have to work at keeping the tide of your emotions back. Only the true recognition of the man's love as words and actions in the moment, and often, is going to do it. Otherwise you'll seethe in your silence and lack of giving.

How can you expect him to acknowledge his loving feelings in making love to you when you can't acknowledge his love when he is loving you as I've described above? Do you see the connection here? You must give first to receive. That's the law in love.

I'd say you have a good chance, after eight years, of rediscovering the love and rightness that has actually kept you together. But you have to make yourself lovable by giving up your selfish self-consideration. You don't have to call him, 'dearest, darling Tom' when you're not sure you mean it. Why not simply say to him, with a straight face and no attempt to emotionalise or project, 'I love you Tom. I know I love you Tom. I mightn't or sometimes can't feel it but I know it's true. I trust you can hear me and love me through my emotions. I'm taking responsibility for them Tom. I'm not going to put them on you and I'm not going to think about them. If I should feel myself failing, may I just come to you and ask you to question me so that I might face up to being responsible for them with your help?'

Man can only love a woman, be with a woman, because she gives him pleasure, gives him herself. You are giving him not yourself but your unhappiness. If you continue he will leave you. Or such a gap will grow between you that it will represent the same thing. You're the one who has to make yourself lovable, not by trying to be anything but by simply giving up being what you are not.

Now get on with it, woman, and let's get this tragedy of love as it is on earth, right.

Dear Barry

I'm very confused in a few areas of my life. One is my relationship to my partner, the other area is master-disciple relationship.

I feel I don't trust my partner any more. I'm feeling hurt by him. I'm really feeling lost and emotional as I write, tears coming. My mind says that I create all the problems where none exist. Barry, in the beginning of this relationship I was strong, myself, honest and I knew what was what. And now I've perhaps compromised somewhere and I can't see what's happened or where I am. I need help.

I feel that I need to make clear my relationship with you. Who are you in relationship with me? You have come into my life in the past at very crucial times. I have listened and meditated to your tapes and amazing things have happened. Also I have listened and found the tapes boring and they say nothing at all. Barry, when I have doubts they wreck me, yet I have them. I get into despair at having nothing, not even a master. I used to feel you were my internal master reflecting to me the truth outside of me. Then I feel I have dependency on seeing you regularly or I lapse into misery.

Another question: I have heard you say that woman knows when she is loved by man and she should feel loved all the time, not only for half an hour in the day. I asked my mother about this point and she said it had nothing to do with the other person — the man that is. I think she meant self love but I thought you meant that my partner should be loving to me, honest, real and that when I as a woman was truly loved, I would know it in my bones. Can you clarify this for me?

Barry, in all spiritual teachings they emphasise a guru or master. Today I was reading parts of a book by Swami Saraswati Satyananda and he was describing various master-disciple relationships. I was a sannyasin of Rajneesh for several years but I feel, seeing I get so stuck and doubtful, that not much went in. It all comes and goes. What I feel I want is something solid and honest in my life. I seem to go backward, get worse, not better or clearer.*

A month ago I spoke to you about reality and my partner smoking marijuana and cigarettes. After talking and listening to you, I felt good and right. But nothing happened.

So, can you read the lines and between the lines and let me know if God made me faulty or what I am doing wrong.

I have discovered also that I don't like people, that I look at every man as a sexual prospect or not, always looking for someone better to love. Is this an immaturity in me? Also I see other women as competition — the prize being man. Therefore I don't have friends and I don't really want them, unless for something I need in the moment.

Another problem has come up to ask you. I stopped smoking five months ago, partly due to seeing you at the Teaching Week. I felt I couldn't be the truth and smoke any more and it's been great to stop. Since then I have put on weight. I feel it is keeping me from feeling myself just like the smoking did. Is it because I'm not being loved enough that I eat more for nourishment and so I won't be attractive any more and won't be loved for sure?

One last thing: my partner and I have been following

the 'Making Love' tapes and I have come across so much hate, violence and pain, sometimes I don't know if it is now or past. I feel my partner tricks me sometimes. He doesn't ejaculate when we make love but he masturbates to release his tension. I find this a bit distressing.

I feel I will stop now. I can see I have a lot inside not right at the moment. Please help if you can and by God if you answer — be honest.

Shanti

* Sannyasin: traditionally a Hindu renunciate but in this context a disciple of Bhagwan Shree Rajneesh, later Osho, an Eastern master who advocated sexual freedom as part of his teaching.

Shanti

You say, 'and by God if you answer — be honest'. So now you get what you're looking for.

If Shanti is your sannyasin name, change it back to what it was. Accept responsibility for yourself; let all your sannyasin past go. It is the cause of many of your problems.

For instance, 'I look at every man as a sexual prospect or not, always looking for someone better to love'. Also, 'I see other women as competition — the prize being man'. This is the legacy of your sannyasin years when you were not taught the difference between sex/emotion/excitement and love. Every man you had in the sannyasin club poured his sexual ignorance/restlessness into you. And now you drum with sexual discontent and competitiveness that is not of you, not of woman, but of manipulative man. The club manipulated you for man's sexual excitement and numerous other women like you, and now like an emotional pregnancy it lives in your stomach. You will feel it distinctly start rising and drumming in you — wanting, seething for some sort of satisfaction or gratification of the old sexual excitement.

Woman is the receptive principle and she becomes what man puts into her. She is also pure love (before man gets at her) and as love she lives to please her love — man. So put her in a club where the rule is for the men to dip in 'to remove her blockages' or some other spurious truth related to God or love — and she will do her best to be true and to please until she herself gets infected or pregnant with the same devilish predatory energy. Self-doubt, unsourceable discontent and all the rest of it then arise.

Of course, Rajneeshis are not the only victims of this errant, undisciplined energy. Wherever there has been permissive or promiscuous sex as a practice and certainly as spiritual experimentation or therapy, the psychic possession will be found. But tragically all around the world I have found it more embedded as a rule in Rajneeshi men and women. Tragic because the more serious ones, having been in the master's presence, possess a receptivity and openness to the truth but this becomes clouded over; tragic also because the effects, especially on the woman, sap her authority and power, exposing her to continual sexual and emotional manipulation by members of the club.

So you write to me in despair from that place and still looking for another guru to mislead you, preferably perhaps an Indian. You must throw out all gurus as any sort of image — and if you have a mala* that's the first symbol to get rid of.

So what else are you to do to get out of it?

Listen to the truth where you hear it. Do not believe anyone or anything — especially not gurus or eastern masters. And don't believe Barry Long either. You have been through all you have to this date to gather experience of ignorance, dishonesty and delusion. You've done it. You're up to your neck in it. You know it, first hand in your own experience. It has all been God-given so you can know what you do not want. So now you can use your authority — knowing what you don't want.

Do you want a man who doesn't love you? That's what you've got. Do you want a man who smokes marijuana or cigarettes? Do you want a man who practises part of my teaching (the good part like my 'Making Love' tapes) but not the hard part like being honest with you 24 hours a day? Do you want a man who masturbates — once he has been told that masturbation ceases once fantasising over sex/woman is abandoned? Do you want a partner that you do not trust? You may feel you love him — and why not? But that's not the point now. Which is the biggest 'yes'? Do you want to continue to be unhappy as you clearly are? If the answer is no, leave him. Not because I say so but because you are at last responsible for yourself, for love, and see the truth. Never look back and never complain.

Go somewhere, away from Rajneeshism and all that past that is hanging round your neck like the mala you once wore. Be alone. Dry out. Go celibate. The energy will give you hell. It will hate you, it will hate me. It will make you feel like killing yourself, like an abysmal failure and utterly useless. But you won't be either. It will just be trying to break your resolve by getting some of the old club satisfaction. You are not that woman any more.

You must know what you do not want. If the other person is giving you what you do not want and they will not change, you must leave them. What they want to do is their business. What effect it has on you is your business.

Don't blame. Just quit.

You eat more because you are not loved. You smoked for the same reason and eating is just a substitute. It is better, once both have done all they can, to leave and be alone than to be together and not loved. Don't carry the non-love into the aloneness. Once you break you will be new. And eventually, as you wring the past out of you (or it is wrung out of you), you will draw to yourself a man of sufficient love to love you. It will take time. Don't be misled by the wolves that will try to follow you.

In all that I have written here, know that I do not tell you what to do. I simply reply to your letter and give you what you asked for. The truth is only the truth if it is true in your experience. In that, indeed, I am guru — if you hear me. I am not a master to be followed, placed on a pedestal or enshrined in a picture or image. I am the living truth that speaks forever and am either heard or not heard according to your lights.

Yes, woman, when you are truly loved you know it in your bones, for you are love. Do not settle for less or you will ache.

* Mala: a beaded necklace with an image of Rajneesh, worn by his disciples.

[Two and a half months later Barry wrote to Shanti again.]

Shanti

You asked for help and I responded.

Why have you not replied?

[Her reply followed a few days later.]

Dear Barry

Last night I felt I could finally write to you and let you know what happened after your letter. And then today I got your note asking why I hadn't replied. So now I can't avoid writing.

Your letter sunk in — in time. Immediately though I dropped the old name. You were right about letting go of the past. Your letter was just the push I needed. You were right about everything. I carried your letter with me everywhere and I felt all would reveal itself — what I would need to do.

I went to your week's teaching on my own and knew I had to leave my partner when I got back home. It was obvious for me, I was feeling lighter without him.

Now I'm on my own. I have a little cottage by the sea. It happened so fast me being here. My partner sensed the change was coming. He hasn't resisted, he has helped me. He's let me go. I did a lot of crying but I can still feel the love and space. I can see we have been true to the situation, not necessarily to enjoyment. I created a lot of mental prisons around my relationship, burdening both of us. Now we both have space.

Since the Teaching Week I feel I have a steadiness and a stillness in me and to be honest with you I feel loved that you asked me to reply. Hard to let love in — but not really, I'm doing my best. I have a lot less emotion in me since being with you.

You are right about the past being wrung out of me and I can see how important it is. What is real will still be there.

Since leaving what was my home, I find it hard to actually think here in this new place. I realise thinking creates structures around me and I don't know if I want that any more. I can see my mind is scared to think. I also can't see past today. Everything you said in reply to my letter I experienced as the truth and seeing it have acted on all of your advice, even though making the changes has taken me into unknown but knowable places. Perhaps I'll freak out but maybe I won't. I can feel a trust in me, in my life.

When I am at your meetings I experience that you receive my gratitude because I feel so intensely, like grace descending on me. There is tingling all over. Perhaps it is the 'glory' you mention in 'Stillness is the Way'.

You have never let me down when I asked for help and you are honest. I acknowledge you.

Thank you for the privilege of writing back to you. Forgive me if I'm so soppy.

Lynne (formerly Shanti)

Lynne

Well done. And well done by your partner too.

Man and woman must learn to serve God. God is love and love is letting go — when prisons begin to form between us.

Now you still serve God by being honest, true to life, as you have expressed it — for God is also life.

❖

You eat more because you are not loved; you smoke for the same reason

Dearest Barry

I am living the divine life as much as I do and life is truly fortunate and I've been blessed in so many ways. The thing is I'm addicted to several substances: cigarettes, alcohol and on weekends, intravenous speed.

What makes me unhappy is the guilt. My addiction is something I'm observing and aware of and I know it has to go. But it's the guilt and trips about it that seem to be the first barrier. If you could comment on that to me it would be a great help. Thank you for being.

Judith

Judith

Your obsession with the substances you describe is due to the bad company you are keeping and your lack of being loved. The latter comes first and the bad company of others who are afraid to love or be loved follows. Birds of a feather still flock together. Break your attachment and association with these people or friends, first. Then, love man physically but not for sex or with sex-orientated man. He must love you. The substances and friends associated with them are substitutes for love — the manifestations of fear.

You should be ashamed of yourself, not guilty. Weekend intravenous speed? Disgraceful. Your guilt is an excuse for your shameful behaviour. Feel guilty and do it again! What delusion, what self-indulgence. You asked for it. Now get rid of your friends.

Dear Barry

I am writing because I have a problem in my life and need some personal words from you, or more to the point, I need to tell you of my problem. I overeat and often after doing so I make myself sick. The medical profession call this bulimia.

I have been doing this on and off over ten years. I do it to escape right suffering, to escape facing the void within. My mind is very clever at persuading me to eat too much. It's as if to stay in the moment is so awful that I have to have this anaesthetic, food. Then I can always make it all right by bringing it back up — horrible, yes, I am ashamed. I have always thought, 'today it will go' but ten years later it is still the major problem in my life. I know I must stop. I want to stop, which is why I am writing to you. I have tried therapists and doctors but my mind always creates a get-out clause. I have always felt too ashamed to ask for your help on this and my mind has always persuaded me it will go. But no, I may stop for months on end but always I come back to this habit of escape. Maybe I am addicted to the wrong suffering but I don't want it any more. I have started daily meditation again and take regular exercise.

I have a right relationship and two beautiful children. My outward life is right for me but with this major addiction I have, I feel rather like an alcoholic. Can you write some words to me? I pray life may grant me my power to be true and suffer rightly.

I know you are very busy with letters and writing and talks etc but I ask you to send me a few words.

Sally

Sally

Anorexia is caused by a lack of love. Its logical extension bulimia is rooted in shame. Shame, and love as a problem, are associated with sex. These are simply definitions to lay the ground for you. There are no problems on earth that are not associated with lack of love perceived in oneself or apprehended in another.

You say that you have a right relationship and that your outward life is right for you which I assume means that they are not causing you any worry or concern. This I accept.

Your problem is shame. You are ashamed of something in the past. Twice in your letter you mention the word in association with the bulimia. But that shame is a red herring, an effect, like the bulimia itself, and not the cause. Nevertheless the use of the word twice is your subconscious way of communicating the truth to me, underneath that tricky conscious mind you mention, and which insists on calling itself I. It even says 'I am addicted. . .' You are not addicted. You are deeply troubled and that pinching emotion goes back to perhaps six or nine months before the bulimia started.

I want you to look very closely at that time which, from your letter, must be around 11 years ago. Look for some traumatic, emotionally painful event.

Your clever mind will try to hide the event from you; it will not want to 'suffer' the pain of seeing the truth. This mind is really the wilful and cowardly self which spoils everybody's life in some way or other by obscuring the truth. The reason is that the mind or self thrives in the darkness of concealment and dies or vanishes in the light of openness and honesty. So you are right when you say 'I do it to escape right suffering, to escape facing the void within'; but it is the mind again there calling itself I, and it is not the facing of the void which is troubling it on this occasion, but the facing of the root pain of its existence which is your shame.

What are you ashamed of Sally? What have you forgotten because it is just too painful to remember?

❖

Barry Long

Please help me. It's very wicked to say, but I don't know how much longer I can go on. I seem to be heading uncontrollably to self destruction. I'm actually killing myself by the way that I'm living. Please help me.

In the summer after I'd seen you things were different. My life changed for a few months and I knew love and being and true happiness in being alive. Then in October/November I felt things change; there was a barely perceptible 'something' trying to get in. I really fought this with everything I had for a time, but since Christmas I lost the battle. I know it's my fault. I couldn't hold it.

Barry, there's no love in me, not even for those dearest to me. I have an eating disorder which vanished in the summer but which returned with such violence that I'm afraid I may actually be seriously ill. I eat and eat and cannot stop even when I feel sick and my stomach hurts. I've gained a stone in weight in three weeks. I find myself completely disgusting and utterly repulsive. I cannot make love any more. I do not love and I cannot receive the love that those around me are trying to give me. Please, please how do I get out of this dark dark hell?

Jody

PS Strange really, as you can see I'm in a bit of a state to say the least, but I've just been out to hang up the washing and it's so wonderful out there. You know, however despairing I get, the nature out there never leaves. It throbs inside me and strikes the deepest chord of beauty in me. There's an indescribable softness in the air; the birds are singing a song of sheer gladness and although the sky is grey there's a brightness somehow. I can't believe I can still feel this pain when life is so rich. There's no problem here alone, it's just I can't seem to get it straight with those closest to me. I don't seem to be able to understand, however hard I try. The more I seek to understand and control my life, the more of a tangle I seem to get in.

Jody

You must face the fact. There is something fundamentally disturbing between you and the person closest to you. When you say, 'I can't seem to get it straight with those closest to me', you are talking about one person most. When you say, 'I don't seem to be able to understand, however hard I try', I'm asking you why do you need to understand the other person at all?

The situation is that you are unhappy. There is nothing to understand about this. And you are unhappy with what that person is doing to you or not doing. What you have to do is be honest. What is it?

What happened in October/November? What actual event took place that disturbed you within? It may have been small and of no apparent consequence but you must find it and say what it was to start to see what you are afraid to face or are hiding from. Your eating problem is due to a perceived lack of being loved as you know love to be. You are making excuses, blaming and criticising yourself, instead of facing up to the fact of life — the one fact that is making you miserable.

I suggest that it is in the home or family and probably

exacerbated by an event that happened at Christmas when you gave up.

But when you go outside the home or the family, as you write in the postscript, to hang up the washing, you see life is so beautiful and describe it to me with the perception of the love of God.

You can get out of this hell, as you describe it, by being honest to yourself and not trying to live what you are not.

[She wrote back a few weeks later.]

Barry Long

Thank you for your letter. It has helped me to open my eyes to my situation, but more than that it has done something energetic in my life. I realise that all my life I have refused to face facts by blaming myself. I am now facing the fact of my unhappiness and realise that my love-life is unhappy. My husband has always been so good to me, but his patience and wonderful kindness have all been directed at the little girl in me and not at the woman that I really am. I am praying now to be united with this woman.

The difficulty is that I cannot make love. For a long time my husband and I have been listening to the 'Making Love' tapes and practising as often as we can, but I find myself suddenly unable to do this any more. This goes further than mere dislike — I am actually revolted to the point of nausea by it. For me to continue to override my feelings and mechanically go through making love in the vague 'hope' that if I practise doing as the tapes say long enough everything will come right, has become intolerable to me. It isn't right, Barry. It's not working. Making love — even your way — has just become an extension of all the other duties that my femininity has thrust upon me from making beds to cleaning up kids. Don't think I'm angry at you, Barry, because I know you can help me in becoming this beautiful woman that I know is somewhere inside. It's just at the moment I feel like a rare and wonderful bird of paradise that has got caught in a cage and I'm looking for the key — if not I'll smash my way out somehow!

You know, I had this beautiful thing happen to me yesterday that made me know there's more. I spoke briefly to a neighbour, a man of great stillness. The simpering 'little girl disguise' is usually very shy and fluttery with men, but yesterday I was feeling too depressed to be bothered to pretend and for that brief encounter with the neighbour, the woman managed to come out. Something bordering on the exquisite passed between us. I felt so deep and so still, so beautiful inside. The space enclosing us both was as vast and dark as an immense cathedral. The moment was so tender and so sacred that I felt the urge to place one exquisitely beautiful kiss upon his cheek. I hardly know this man and I certainly don't 'fancy' him. I got the feeling that who he was was quite irrelevant! I'm laughing, Barry, I'm quite, quite mad — it's just that it is even madder to carry on as things were. If this experience is just a small taste of how things can be between man and woman, then, Barry, I believe you. But what do I do about — the husband, the tapes, the love-making?

Love (because I am)

Jody

Jody

This is what has happened and is happening in your life — and in your subconscious where I work to bring those who are ready and willing, like yourself, closer to God, purity or freedom. I'm going to read your letter to you from behind the words you wrote. Behind the words, behind the appearance, behind the manifested actions, is the truth.

First, my letter, as you say, opened your eyes, energetically helping you to realise, at last, that your love-life is unhappy; that the little girl in woman loves indulgence and settles for compromise to get it while the woman in her despises such immature impurity.

For a long time, you say, you and your husband have been listening to my 'Making Love' tapes and practising, and now you find yourself 'suddenly unable' to make love with him any more. What did you think you were practising making love with the tapes for?

The tapes are subconsciously energetic and they serve two purposes. One is to break through the familiarity and habit that prevent a couple from enjoying once again the physical love-making they had in the beginning, and the other is to reveal whether the love was founded in love or in some attempt to escape the pain of the past already inside you when you met.

The second option is what has happened to you. You have travelled down the love you've been making to the pain of woman underneath — the pain of not having been loved rightly or sufficiently. So you now say it has become intolerable 'for me to continue to override my feelings and mechanically go through making love in the vague hope that if I practise doing what the tapes say long enough everything will come right'.

Everything has come right. You have discovered that you do not love your husband in the physical way that you always thought. The truth has set you free. You cannot go on loving that way with that man. He does not love you enough — or you don't love him enough. Either way it's intolerable. When you say making love, even my way, has just become an extension of all the other domestic duties, you have missed the point: that making of love my way was the thing that revealed the truth to you. So you say almost contradictorily, 'I know you can help me in becoming this beautiful woman that I know is somewhere inside'.

You know that because the process is still going on. So you add, 'It's just at the moment I feel like a rare and wonderful bird of paradise that has got caught in a cage and I'm looking for the key — if not I'll smash my way out somehow'.

So the rare and beautiful bird (which you'll find referred to in my 'Journal One') now stands revealed, naked, in your consciousness, your body. She walks outside shining psychically — woman, now open to the love of man, freed of the caging love of husband and domesticity.

What happens?

She speaks to a neighbour — 'a man of great stillness' — the man in him reflecting her new need of man's love untainted by the familiarity and casualness of the past which had encased her. She feels 'the urge to place one exquisitely beautiful kiss upon his cheek', a man she 'hardly knows'. 'The simpering little girl disguise' she usually adopts of 'being very shy and fluttery with men' has gone. For once she is woman. 'I'm laughing, Barry, I'm quite, quite mad.' It's a song of joy, of freedom found, not of despair or fear.

And she says, 'I certainly don't fancy him — I got the

feeling that who he was, was quite irrelevant!' Yes, woman, the truth is it does not matter who he is. It only matters that he is man and that you in the moment see his beauty (if you do) — and love him.

Love him? What does such love mean? You know what it means, Jody. You want this man in this exquisite moment to love you, for you to take him physically into your body so that you consume one another and unite in the ecstasy of love without choice, without consideration, without identification, without past.

That is where you are. But will you do it? That is not an injunction. It is the everlasting, ever-present question of love. Do you love enough in the moment to be free as love is free? To honour love with all you are when it is there? Or is fear the measure or cage of our love? When fear goes, through the shattering of the past, am I real enough to be the freedom I have so long yearned for and which is now before me?

And finally you ask me, 'if this experience is just a small taste of how things can be between man and woman, then, Barry, I believe you. But what do I do about — the husband, the tapes, the love-making?'

You read my letter. You see. You know.

But in love, in the freedom of love that you have glimpsed, there are no answers, no handy solutions. You must do what you do, do what you know. I can tell you no more.

❖

Dear Barry

As you know, while I was attending your seminars in Europe I managed to stop smoking. But when I returned to my home and work I started again. My relationship with Vincent became less and less loving. After a couple of months I found that I did not know if I wanted to go on living with him. After we had talked about it and when I still did not know what to do, he started to talk about my smoking. All the time he wanted to tell me to quit smoking or he would leave me. Eventually he gave me the ultimatum and after a while I told him I would try to stop again.

Well, to cut a long story short, I did not know if we could take each other any further and if the best thing was to break up. I did not manage to stop smoking. Vincent became very sick, superior, difficult to communicate and live with but did not leave me.

Maybe we had better leave each other at once? Why is it so hard to see what to do? Is all this about my smoking? We have not been making love very often over the last few months but when we do everything feels better.

There is no smile and openness in Vincent right now. I also feel that he puts it on me when I try and point out where he's not being straight. If he cannot see it in himself and I ask him to look again, he explains in a very smart, verbal and spiritual way. We have even started to have arguments! And I am still smoking!

A good thing is that I managed to fast for the first time in my life. I have started to lose weight.

Heidi

Heidi

Energy you are wasting in the living of your life is needed to change or start transforming your life — that is, to bring your life together into a harmonious whole. In your case, the most easily identifiable leak of energy is through the smoking habit/attachment. Also the food. Which can you deal with first? I said smoking. But perhaps it's the other way round. Overcoming the eating fixation/habit may provide the energy to address or stop smoking. You have to start somewhere. It means, either way, self-denial. Fasting, I have to say, is not a cure. It is a delusive palliative fostered by women's magazines etc and it makes woman (and man) unhappier than they were because, except in rare cases, after the fast she fails and starts eating up again till the next desperate fast. The cure is mastery every meal of the intake habit so that food becomes moderate, like breathing.

For you and Vincent to split is of course an option. But I suggest you split with smoking first. Have you got your priorities right, Heidi? Which do you love, smoking or Vincent? If you love smoking first then Vincent of course is going to feel cheated on, unappreciated, unloved. And he will become hard to protect himself from the hurt of being second best to a fag. If you split with Vincent, does the evidence suggest this will cure your smoking or food habit? I think not. But if you split with tobacco the evidence seems to point to a closer union with the man you apparently love. For man came first before any other love she acquired.

It is not easy breaking with an acquired or unnatural love; harder sometimes than breaking with the real thing. I am with you both in your endeavour to be true to what you know to be true.

Barry Long

I have been with this teaching for two years now. The energy of the words has awakened me to the beautiful feeling of myself. I feel my own love within. I continue to climb the mountain of myself. I have not made physical love with a man for some years; the opportunity to have sex has been given.

I cannot give myself to sex ever again. I feel great gratitude to the love you are, that has awakened me to the love that I am. The energy of the words are within me.

I have not idolised you, nor do I think of you. My question: I long to make physical love with you. This does not cause me pain or suffering. The longing is for union with the male principle that is love. You are that.

I am aware I am layered with emotion, stiff. This longing does not feel like that emotion. This longing feels like my natural state. Why, Barry, do I particularly long to make love with you? Would you please tell me.

Veronica

[She wrote again ten days later.]

Barry Long

In one of your tapes, you say, fear is a protection, yet the fear must be faced eventually in the moment. I cannot reach the state of consciousness that I am whilst I have this desperate, overpowering need for food and cigarettes.

I feel a strange emptiness within, without these things.

My mouth is never free. I am aware of this in me now, as if I am watching me. I am a well rounded woman. I delight in my body, yet I succumb to the thinker that troubles itself with image and pressure from the world to be thin. When I use force and try to stop I feel tremendous pressure and trying. As I am stiller the emotion becomes even more greedy and wanting. I have been celibate for many years. I am vulnerable to love not sex. The need for these things lived in me before I became celibate. The strongest longing is to cleanse myself of this emotion that creates the need for these things, or anything. Would you advise me, and may I write again and ask for more?

Thank you.

Veronica

Veronica

No, you may not write to me again and ask for more. In that last sentence of your second letter you define the cause of your problem and prescribe the treatment. The answer to the question is always in the question itself.

The greedy emotion you describe is living off your need to have some more. From now on it has to be enough for you to have enough. So every time you want some more — having had some or enough — don't.

There is no magical answer to your problem. You have to do it. You have to deny your self which is your greed. You must say no as you say you have said no to sex. Your greed for food and for another cigarette is sex in another form.

You must be aware in your life every time you want some

more. You will find it common in many subtle ways other than in the desire for food or nicotine. If you want to make another phone call — don't. If you want to tell someone something because you feel you haven't made the point sufficiently — don't. If you feel the need to fill up your petrol tank when it's not necessary — don't.

It's not the pressure from the world that makes you want to be thin. It's the knowledge of the truth in you that you are indulging yourself and that you have the power to neutralise this possession. Not by fighting or trying, which is the irresponsible way, but by knowing why you are not giving in to the greed — by being responsible for it. At present you are making out as though the greed was something separate from yourself. It's not. It is yourself. So you'd better get hold of yourself, get hold of it in the little things before it grows into the monster of the two big things you choose to mention.

You may write to me in three months time and tell me how you have succeeded by denying yourself in all the little 'unimportant' things. Everyone wants to give up the big problem, not realising that it is an accumulation of all the little problems they indulge so many times a day.

About asking to make love with me. There you go again. You feel great gratitude to the love I am that has awakened you to the love that you are — and then you ask for more. It's not the asking that's the problem. It's the need to ask.

I love She,
am united with her
in the love of God,
as man

❖

I challenge you Barry Long.

You are man. You cannot know the love that is woman or the pain of her suffering.

You have said, 'Woman cannot do what I do' but a woman must do what you do for woman, for the love that she is.

You may think you know woman but you are not She.

Holly

Holly

You ungrateful woman. Why do you need to challenge me? What have I done to you to warrant such an outburst of your independence, your pain?

Have I not helped you? Have I asked anything of you for myself in all my answers to your cry for truth and love? Do I not serve woman, do my best to help free her of the acquired lovelessness you have directed towards me?

No, I am not She. But I love She, am united with her in the love of God, as man. And inasmuch as She is in a woman, She hears me and loves me for my endeavour to reach her, to free her.

Write me of your love, not of your spleen. Or be gone and live with it.

❖

He loves you, yes — but does he love you enough?

Dear Barry

I have been with your teaching for several years now and I thank God for bringing me to you. Your teaching is a delight to me and I realise its rightness and truth more and more as my life unfolds. So first I want to thank you for doing what you do, being who you are, and 'telling it like it is'.

I am always able to feel the wellbeing inside my body even at the times of greatest agitation and suffering in my life, yet despite this I cannot trust that life will look after me. My greatest fear at the moment is that I will be alone and have no man to love.

My partner has been with the teaching for a few years. Immediately he came into your presence all doubts about the truth of who you are vanished and he accepts the teaching totally.

Unfortunately, although he accepts the teaching he seems very unwilling to live it and our relationship is under very great strain. In fact life is hell and I feel that if I don't leave I will lose my sanity.

Even though he is committed to your teaching, at the moment he says he feels very estranged from it and is refusing to listen to your tapes. It is fatal for me to say anything about what you teach regarding relationships (even though I apply it to myself as well) because he just says that it's okay for you because you're Barry Long!! I must say I am not throwing Barry Long at him every two minutes but I try to make him realise the truth that I've heard and want to live with him.

I would like to tell you what he is doing in our relationship at the moment which causes me such anguish, because I don't know any more how much of my reaction is from self and how much is the working through of life.

He says he cares for me but doesn't love deeply — this applies to everyone that he says he loves.

My body is a problem at the moment because he told me he dislikes it (I'm in my mid forties and I've gone a bit flabby in places — it is this he doesn't like). I reacted very emotionally when he told me this. It was also a relief because I knew there was 'something' causing a problem even though at first he denied it. I know this is my self — I understand reaction and response and that this has struck a very raw nerve in myself. But I worry it like a dog with a bone — in fact I am pathetic about it and keep referring to it in our relationship.

He tried to make me (and himself) believe that he had dealt with 'this judgement of my body' (his words) and it was no longer there. He did this twice and both times he admitted he'd lied and it was still there. So now I don't know what is the truth for him regarding me and what isn't.

He says this dislike of your partner's body is very common and it is just because 'I'm a man in our culture'. It is not so much the criticism about my body that is the problem, although it is hard for me to accept, it's the barriers to love — both from him and me — that are now erected.

Also he won't talk to me. Sometimes (I am not always emotional) I calmly tell him how I feel about this situation, and he just won't reply to me. In fact he often becomes very sleepy and goes to sleep when I talk to him. If I never mentioned any of our problems again and just generally chatted to him I am sure everything would go back to normal — but I can't live with the dishonesty.

All this makes me want to leave the relationship (we

have been together for 15 years) but something keeps me here. I know that there is still love for him in me (although it has taken a great battering) and I tell myself it's because 'it's not finished yet' that I stay. But I am afraid that I will never meet another man and will be on my own for the rest of my life and I also wonder if it's this fear that is keeping me in this very unhappy relationship. In other words that the fear of being alone is the real reason why I stay and all the other thinking is delusion.

I am so sorry to have written such a long letter. Please don't think I am just wanting to catalogue my partner's shortcomings to you. I think now that it is not healthy or acceptable for me to want him to change. It's me that doesn't know what to do about the situation and I just can't live with it.

Once again, Barry, I am sorry this letter is so long and I know how busy your life is. I hope that the physical act of writing to you will set some truth in motion in my life and so I thank you for being there.

With deep love to the master.

Margaret

Margaret

What can you do?

First, when a man tells a woman he does not like her body she must do what is obvious: not allow him to enter it until he changes his critical perception. To allow him to use her body when it suits him is a denial of the love and consciousness she craves for; and is a demonstration on his part that he is divided in his love to the extent of being two-faced. In both cases the truth is not served and the lie of an unhappy relationship continues.

You say your partner accepts my teaching totally. This is rubbish, intellectual theorising. To accept the teaching is to practise it, live it. And you can't select parts of it to live. Total means all. There are no specialists in any aspects of my teaching. It is a total life of self-abnegation. His self is

- refusing to listen to my tapes;
- critical of my teaching regarding relationships (what the heck are you doing together?);
- refusing to listen to you when you point out his dishonesty, irrespective of where the point is derived from;
- says he cares for you but doesn't love deeply (yet continues to live with you);
- makes the excuse for his likes and dislikes by saying, 'I'm a man in our culture' (this is an example of not being a man and of not taking responsibility for himself);
- won't talk to you;
- becomes sleepy and goes to sleep when you endeavour to speak to him of your problems.

Second, you can leave him. Since you describe it as hell, do you see hell getting any better? I'd say what you've described is living death, which I suppose is another description of hell. If you know it is not healthy or acceptable for you to want him to change, then it's you who'll have to do something about it.

Third, you must not look to the future beyond the first action to take. That will create fear. You must free yourself of this situation first before you can even consider what will happen next — particularly regarding whether you'll be left all alone.

I do not tell anyone what to do. You have asked my advice and on the facts you've given me I have responded. My teaching is to make man an honest and noble creature (as he was in the beginning) by his taking responsibility for his dishonest and ignoble self and having no more of it; and to return woman to being the intelligence of love that does not compromise with man's unhappy self or her own doubts and fears, as she was in the beginning.

This letter is not a criticism of your partner or you. It is the statement for anyone who can see the truth of it in the mirror of their relationship.

❖

Dear Barry

My partner and I often come to your meetings. I hear the truth you speak and am endeavouring to live it. I am urged to write to you, the problem being jealousy in my relationship. I don't know what to do.

I love my partner and want to be with him but over the some three years of our relationship the jealousy in him keeps raising its ugly head and literally explodes. He says he doesn't know why he feels this jealousy. I in turn won't have it and keep sending him away until he looks at it, but he can't or won't.

It is myself I struggle with. I don't want a jealous partner and yet I love him. My confusion is so intense as to what to do, could you say something about that?

At this moment of letter writing we are apart. I am not unhappy. I want it right. What can I do for both of us?

I thank you for reading my letter.

Celia

Celia

A jealous man is an unhappy man and if he has no good reason to be jealous of you he has no right to his particular unhappiness.

What is he unhappy about? He has to be honest enough to say what it is. The jealousy is a smokescreen — that's why it's irrational. What is his secret envy or his secret doubt of himself? I suggest it arises from his teenage years — that he hasn't let go of some uncertainty or insecurity of those years and as a result (in that respect) has not grown up.

This is not to blame the man — but he should look at what I'm saying very closely. Help him by asking questions.

While this thing is in him it will always come between you. As it has now at the time of your writing.

An unhappy man will make you unhappy. It's as simple as that, no matter how much you love him. He has to love you enough to find the cause. It is in his past.

❖

Hello Barry Long

I've been to see you twice and I never had the courage to get up in front of you and face myself. This is about me and my boyfriend. We've been together for three years more or less. We've been with Rajneesh, Osho, for many years. Now we are listening to your tapes and it looks like I haven't gone any deeper into myself. I'm the same as I was at 20 and I'm 30 now. I am having sexual problems and difficulties with my boyfriend.

For the last few months I have been either rejecting him sexually or avoiding the making of love. I realise I have never really known what love is. I am afraid to say I love him and I have stopped making love with him.

It is like there is a barrier inside me, that when the happiness arises to a point I say, 'Enough, I can't go over it'. He feels more and more frustrated and whenever he starts feeling good, again this monster inside comes and destroys the beauty.

We've been talking and talking. I don't know what to do but go on putting my meditation on this focus. It seems like it's never ending and I feel a screaming inside. I see myself going around and around to the same point. Please tell me something!

I don't want to split but I do want to be happy again. I've got to solve this, otherwise my relationship is going to finish and I don't want that. Please could you tell me where I am going wrong.

Avibha

Avibha

What does your boyfriend do that makes you feel he does not love you? You must face this and then face him with it so that you and he can get it right without emotionalising or blaming each other. Otherwise you will continue to harbour a subconscious hardness towards him. This is interfering with your love-making. Be honest. Be straight. If he doesn't love you enough you will quit sooner or later.

❖

Dear Barry

Can you please say something about birth control? What happens if you follow your love-making tapes and endeavour to move towards pure love, but the man still ejaculates quite often inside the woman? Is it important to learn to control the ejaculation or to move out of the vagina when coming, or, as one is learning to love more, do these things rectify themselves?

I am afraid of getting pregnant in this kind of involuntary way and I just had an abortion that my husband has not yet forgiven me for. He says that if I had more faith in life and wasn't so paranoid about getting pregnant I would not have become pregnant. Is this true?

I would like to have a child after some time but would like us to love each other more first. Is this something I should forget about and if life gives me a baby I'll just have it?

I hope it is possible for you to say something about all this. It is posing quite a problem between me and my husband at the moment and I am so far unable to see a way out of it. Please write if you can.

Thank you and I am happy that you are in my life.

Rose

Rose

It is your life not your husband's. And it is your body — which is your subconscious mind — not his. If you truly love one another you are of one mind and then there is no difference, no problem. My love and I can work anything out together — as long as, or as much as, we are together in love.

You have to examine honestly how much you are together. How much he does love you and you him.

Love in man is to make love for the pleasure and privilege of entering your subconscious, your mystery, your body — and not just for ejaculation. He does not need to ejaculate so often when he makes love to you and it is selfish for him to do so. He can and must learn to move faster in his subconscious, in his body, and not give into the glandular pressure of immature sexual indulgence.

Man's pleasure is in making the love with you, together — not in his ejaculation. Habitual ejaculation is a demand of the immature mentalising man, as demonstrated in the need to masturbate. The immature mental man uses fantasising as a sexual stimulus, creating a dependence on excitement for stimulation. When the man then enters a woman's body, the process works in reverse and the pleasurable stimulation triggers the excitement — which makes him come.

The device used to prevent this by an experienced, though still immature man, is to forcibly control his excitement and ejaculation with his mind — suppression. This, however, is known by the woman's consciousness in her vagina and interferes with the pleasure of her love, her fulfilment, even though she may not consciously entertain the thought. She will, however, feel that something was or is missing. And the man himself will be able to 'grind away' at length without feeling much love in the act. His penis also will become less and less sensitive and therefore increasingly dependent on artificial stimulation.

To answer another one of your questions. Nothing to do with man's sexual love rectifies itself. He has to be responsible for his part, his body.

Why shouldn't you not want to get pregnant? If he loves you enough you would not be reluctant to have his child now. But he doesn't, or you don't believe he does. I quote part of your letter to you, 'I would like to have a child after some time but would like us to love each other more first'.

This does not mean what your conscious mind thinks it means. It was written by your subconscious, your body. It means: 'We do not love each other enough for me to have a (why didn't you say his?) child'. You want a child later when the man (whoever he is) loves you enough.

Your husband hasn't forgiven you for having an abortion? That is lack of love and understanding. You know that. And it is not true what he says about having faith and not getting pregnant. It's not faith in life you have to have, or that you are lacking. It's faith in his love. And you don't have it, do you? How could you when first of all he assumes the divine right to forgive another and immediately abdicates the right by not forgiving.

I trust you can both work this out together in love and not in argument or accusation. If you don't, the lack of love will grow and eventually separate you.

I do not make the rules. I just say it as it is. I am not telling you what to do. Everything is up to you. You asked for my help and that's it.

❖

When sex is faced rightly it eventually returns to the power of love

Barry

I am feeling very confused about the teaching and woman. It feels like woman is being pushed back to a place she's been trying to get out of for hundreds of years. There was a movie I saw once in which women were given pills every day to make them perfect little wives; this has come up for me.

I don't know if you're mad or not. I'm feeling washed out, confused and I'm seeing my man Roger as a brain-washed robot. I've listened to you before and completely trusted you and saw who you were, now I'm having doubts.

I hope you can understand what I'm trying to say.

Cheryl

[She wrote again three days later.]

Barry

You probably read the first letter I sent a few days ago. Well, I'm feeling much softer now and not emotional. I've had time to feel all the stuff going on inside me, all the fear coming up about the changes ahead for me and Roger, all the fear the teaching brings up for me. I don't feel like fighting it any more.

Over the last few days I've seen all the layers of protection I've accumulated all my life and how slowly they are starting to shed, how I never let things affect me. I'm only just feeling the pain now. I'm feeling frightened of making love with Roger in case he's not totally sincere, because I don't want any more sex in me, but we are talking about everything very honestly and that feels good.

In my first letter I said I thought you were crazy but I guess I wouldn't have written to you if I really believed that. Now I've had time to work out some things for myself and I know that you speak the truth and that's why I'm writing to you.

Cheryl

Cheryl

You are going to have those disturbances from time to time. They are inevitable when you focus on me and my teaching. I am love and my teaching is truth. I can say this because I live all that I teach, as one day you must live all that you teach your children or tell others. That is love — to live what you speak or say.

This love, this truth I am, is energetic. It works in the subconscious underneath all the beliefs, opinions and what you think you think. It disturbs the rubbish, the wilful independent self that thinks it knows something of value, when all it knows causes trouble and unhappiness.

My energy disturbs the rubbish so that you can consciously — though invariably, painfully — face it. Facing it slowly dissolves it. The rubbish is the past in you. And its virulence, its destructive potency, is the emotion of attachment to sex in the past.

This sexual emotion lodged in your subconscious consists of two contradictory elements: pain and excitement. These will take turns at pulling at you as you face the emotion.

The pain is the pain of your sexual past that was not love; the excitement is the excitation that accompanied the sexual activity and is still in the emotion in yourself.

I'm now going to discuss the two elements, one at a time: the pain and excitement of the sexual past impinging on the present.

Pain.

The first element is pain/anxiety — like you were in when you wrote your first letter. And the first reaction of the ignorant human mind (as you will see from the letter) is to try to unload the pain onto others by blaming them (for the pain). But the mind being ignorant and not yet enlightened does not realise that the pain is all past. It is the deeply distressing emotional pain you suffered while indulging in sexual freedom and licence in your earlier search for love. Self-indulgence or sex-indulgence like this, especially when encouraged by a spiritual teaching such as Rajneesh sannyas, promises the realisation of love and liberation. But it fails miserably to deliver the goods — the misery being the despairing, exploited women left behind by this male manipulation.

The tragedy, however, is that often the women concerned really think that they are okay and that sexually they are fairly liberated and possibly more liberated than most 'ordinary' women (until such time as they are confronted by my teaching). But this is nothing less than the male manipulative sexuality that has been put into She, the female, and which makes her, for always the best of reasons, continue to indulge in and serve the devilish and rapacious male sexuality — in her own thoughts and physical actions that serve the fantasies of men. She thinks she's in charge when she's already lost.

This servitude to sex requires woman to cut off from her love. Otherwise she could not possibly tolerate being so misused and compulsively driven. To compensate she becomes independent, displaying a hardness that intermittently crucifies her as well as anyone she tries to love, or who tries to love her. You'd got used to feeling hard but in your letter to me you mention you are now feeling soft. This is because I reflect your love to you. And that softness is the natural state of woman. The hardness seeks to promote circumstances which will continue to make you hard, like reasons for cutting off from your partner, or from me or my teaching.

As your life gets righter and improves (which it is, even though at times the hardness may not want to admit it) the sex energy will try to make problems where there are none. It's not going to die overnight. It's a sort of strangulation process — not of you, but of it. So you will suffer less and see more clearly that the sufferer is not you.

You will see some of this quirky independence at work in your first letter where you say you felt 'like woman was being pushed back to a place she's been trying to get out of for hundreds of years'. That may be so. But the fact is you're not being pushed back; you're already there. And you're stuck there (except that I am with you and to the degree that you are with me, you are coming out and you know it). It's the place of your old sexual bondage, the place that you enthusiastically and excitingly embraced for so many years. Man's loveless sexuality was to blame, yes; but you were his willing accomplice in this betrayal of love.

The difference now is that this past is being seen through your growing consciousness of love. That old self, the old cock-sure, hard and independent woman, is being perceived more clearly and separated from, due to my teaching, my energy, my love. This has now entered you and awakened your love, the new woman — she who is dawning in that body out of the dark ignorance of the past.

Excitement.

The second element in the sexual emotion is, as I've said, excitement. This will arise in the independence from time to time as the feeling of 'missing out', or boredom. It is the 'missing' of the old habitual excitement associated with sex in the past. And if the means of indulging the excitement is not there, the feeling is irritability, restless boredom or discontent. And if the means for sexual activity and excitation are there, there will be tension between indulgence and restraint, the latter being the power of developing love to overcome.

The sexual emotion in woman will sometimes be felt as an intense energetic sensation around the abdomen and frequently where there has been promiscuous sex, in the vagina and clitoris. The energy, as it is faced and reduced by the awakening love or consciousness of the woman, often becomes more virulent and seemingly impossible to contain. The woman should be mindful that it is actually a psychic entity or possession living in her subconscious and that the more it is cornered by her stillness and fortitude, the more intensively it will fight.

One of its depressing and dismaying devices is to assail her with ceaseless sexual thoughts and various disturbances and eruptions in the body. These may include rashes like acne, bloating, the eruption of any sexual infections that may have been contracted in earlier years, despairing lack of sleep, loss of weight, stress to a point of gauntness and compulsive activity of some sort. Behind all this there will be an intermittent intense vibration of anxiety — woman's fundamental separation from her love, by sex. Only by the practice of the divine life and through the stillness and service of love, can the woman eventually dissolve or disperse the male sexual invader. Her disturbances will subside and with them will go the possessive force. Through this process she will progressively realise a greater union with love, stillness or God. The intensity of this process varies from woman to woman. But every woman who would be united with love must face it to some degree — for every woman has absorbed psychically or physically the male sexual entity.

You have a choice whenever you think you want one. You can quit focusing on me and go the independent way. You will then be back where you were — hoping that love will come and save you. Since it is already here you will have chosen to leave it and it could be a long wait indeed before it manifests again.

Really though, Cheryl, you have no choice. The love in you does not want one. The self in you that must die, does. And the self is now the lesser part.

While you love me, focus on me and my teaching, all will go increasingly well for you. You will discover that the parts (of your life) fit together with amazing grace. This is the grace of God, the Most High, not me; but I, through the privilege of being a world teacher, have this power. In between, it may be hard and exhausting at times — it being the struggle with your rebelling and independent self. But it will pass, as all things pass but love.

❖

Barry

There is a situation in my life that I have been delaying and delaying in dealing with, wanting to see what to do.

Last year my ex-lover Bruce got someone to spy on me and eventually they supplied him with the names of two men I was seeing. With this information he proceeded in his skilful manipulative way to undermine me and question my sanity. Fortunately, with the help of a friend, I was able to stay in command and use the situation to show him I was not the frail little woman he had endeavoured to turn me into.

I have my suspicions as to who the spy is but the question is, do I raise a hornet's nest by confronting this person or do I leave well alone?

It's horrible, Barry! I have had to learn to be suspicious to live with man. It disturbs my love even now. There is no point in facing Bruce with all this — I have learnt that. He is skilful in turning all situations between us to being the result of my weakness, never his. You talk of man's manipulative ways — well I fell for it and fell for it elsewhere too, until I saw through it with your help.

I'm so tired of it and so tired of all this pain in me. I actually feel sick inside every time I go against my love now and have found myself sobbing with it. I am really working as I never have to get/keep my life clear.

What I dread, Barry, is perhaps (life allowing) being with man again and still having so much mess here to come between me and my love. I love man dearly. How can I be with him bringing all this with me, especially the situation I am writing about? Perhaps I am making a mountain out of a molehill.

Fiona

PS I see that when I write of what can still get in the way of my love, it is because I am not being with my love.

My greatest addiction is daydreaming to escape from the pain of not being with my love (both senses).

The next is self-judgement.

Fiona

While you are afraid of anyone or any condition you will be manipulated.

What have you got to hide that no one should know? Fear gives power to the other, the outer.

Your fundamental fear, the reality you cannot bring yourself to face, is that you are sexually possessed. It is true, as you say, that you love man dearly. And that you are tortured by the pain of not being with it and him. Your addiction is not to daydreaming to escape from the pain, but to your endeavour to reach your love through sexual musical chairs.

Your love is God. God is within. You have put man before God. You now have to put God first. You have to give up sex — making physical love. And you have to give it up willingly by coming back every moment to why you are doing it. I repeat, you are doing it because you have put sexual love before God. This has attracted a possessive psychic addiction to excitement and pain. When the pain of separation (from love that is God) is there you think about sexual thoughts of union. This creates subconscious excitement which drives you to have another try. The excitement gives way to pain. Man rejects you because of the pain. And so the vicious circle continues.

What you are afraid of is what I have said — you are sexually possessed. The prospect of breaking the addiction is like the end of your life to you — or it will be. Your frantic letter suggests that perhaps you're having a taste of it, having to love God or nothing. It is the death of your self, the slow death of your possession. Sex always has something to hide. And lastly it hides from itself. But it cannot hide from me, who is love. So I tell you the truth. You are afraid of being found out, of admitting to your own intelligence your addiction. You know it but you haven't faced it. You project this fear, this hiding, outside yourself to avoid the terrible truth of having to face it. You then blame others for manipulating and spying on you. It is really your own love spying on you, the love of God, the nothing or consciousness within you. You are that but it's too subtle, fine and still against your need of sexual stimulation posing as the love of man.

So get on with it. But be mindful that I am not telling you what to do. You ask for help, for the truth and there you have it — if it is the truth.

Only you can know.

Dear Barry Long

I'm having great difficulty with feelings of guilt and coping with the judgements, hate and anger I feel from Dave about my sexual past. I feel responsible in a way for what he's going through and although I care and want to show him that I do, I seem to be condoning or feeding what he's feeling. Would you please help clarify this?

Joanne

Joanne

You are guilty but not to blame. Your past is yours but the error is you are attached to it. And because he loves you, he has attached himself to it, too. You are in the process of detaching yourselves so you can love one another in the present. Be strong. If you falter and shake, he will. By feeding his self with your honesty you are helping him to destroy his ignorance, his self-ishness.

You are woman, She. In your ignorance, you could not be responsible for your past. But now you can be responsible for your present. Do not feel guilty. You are now honest. Face him. He is facing your past. Make him face your present. Don't make excuses for your past. Just give him the facts. But don't let him make a meal of them and feed his own sexuality — which is what he's doing when he says he can't stand it. All he can't stand is his own self. But don't blame or accuse him. Be the woman you are now.

❖

Dear Barry

Right now I have an enormous lump of pain inside and find it just about impossible to work my way through it. I find myself unable, for a few days now, to do anything but the necessary in housework and childcare. A heaviness weighs me down, my body finds it hard work even to get up physically. All I want to do is sit down and not do anything but when I do that — which is most of the day — I am full of great pain, restlessness and the most violent turmoil in my belly. I seem to sink into a state of madness inside, get engulfed by waves of pain and emotions and thoughts of all kinds. Every now and then I seem to come to the surface for a deep breath before I go down again. All the energy I have seems to be used to hold this thing inside of me in check.

At night I have the most odd dreams of murder and violence and blood and screams of utter despair and pain. I see faces of utmost ugliness with devilish grins while the persons they belong to strangle someone with bare hands or kill them with knives. I see hands dripping with blood and I see the victims that are being murdered or hear their screams. I wander around dark rooms in big houses full of evil and vile-looking people knowing someone's there murdering us all. I see dead bodies and hear bloodcurdling screams in dark corners and rooms.

I wake up with great horror and great fear and am afraid to go back to sleep. Life seems futile and joyless and utter misery. I see pain and unhappiness around me. And in my mind's eye I see this black cloud over me and the world around me — the cloud of negativity that seems to have engulfed me.

It surprised me to come back from your last seminar

and feel all this pain surge in on me. I seemed to feel so good and easy and be filled with love more than ever in your presence. I was hardly disturbed by anything and so delighted in your presence and your words. I felt like I was drinking you in with every fibre of my being. Returning home I seemed to fall into an abyss.

I am since filled with the utmost self-doubt: doubting even whether the love I have felt in the past was real at all, whether I ever really loved or just thought I did, imagined I did. I really don't know what's real at the moment at all. How could I end up like this again? I am fighting a devilish fight of some sort inside without really understanding anything.

Another thing — I keep feeling this pull in my belly, as if I was tied up to you with an elastic band. It's pulling physically (so it seems) at me with such strength at times, that I have to sort of hold on to my body and stay here, as if my body was going to walk right to you out of the door, through the air along the string. It's quite nonsensical I know, but that's how it is with me at the moment. The pull I feel is very painful to me indeed. Do I imagine things? What I do about it is this: I keep sitting down trying to go into Me and disconnect from the thinking (but find I can't). I also keep putting on your tapes. A distant voice keeps telling me it's okay, just something to go through, to be as still with it as I can. It must be right, trust, you are doing your best.

Also what I saw — the loveless monster I have been, the moody, angry, sexual, jealous, blaming etc entity. Gosh. And how the self tries to spoil my true love now when it arises by trying to make myself feel, 'I am "something" now, someone better, I'm really great now, so conscious etc'. It's as if I can't be without my self butting in and either making me feel 'good' or 'bad' about something. Yet all I really want is to be. I experience over and over again the pain it really is to try and be something. I always lose my love when I do, yet I can't stop it happening — yet. My self tries to use even my love to enhance itself ('you look really good now etc'). Of course it's not really surprising looking at how I have fed this self all my life, in utter ignorance of what I was doing. Okay, so I deserve it now, don't I, to have to get rid of it again.

My body hurts. Quite oddly at the seminar (oddly to me that is) my body felt very good in spite of sitting for two days and sitting during the journey there and back — no pain or stiffness. I felt loose and comfortable and flexible. I used to think sitting a lot makes one stiff and aching. Another idea I had that's not true.

A question comes up. After I told you about the urge (or whatever to call it) I often feel to give myself to you and to merge with you, I wondered, what does it really mean to give myself? How do I do it? Isn't it funny that I make a statement like, 'I want to give myself' and then when it comes to it I don't seem to know what it means. It quite shocked me when you said, 'Could you do it?' because I didn't know how and what to actually do — yet it felt like there was something, if only I'd known.

There is still something between me and you — a fear, smaller it seems, but still there. A feeling of being unworthy, a shame about what I am, where I am. Saying 'I love you' to you feels difficult. Does that mean my love is not true? Is there another love I don't know yet? Perhaps my love is still selfish, otherwise why should I feel the way I do. Yet I feel tremendous longing to unite with you across the abyss my self has created — that's the thing I'm looking for, isn't it? — and it's me that creates the barrier, definitely. You are there, you are love, ready to unite and be united with. Is that true what I see there? And I am here striving somehow to get to you. And it's an inner thing — I could sit right next to you and still be separate.

Another day. . .

I feel so much pain. It goes on and on. Is it part of clearing myself or is it just a continuation of ignorance and wrong living? Paul took my daughter, Emma, out. I feel even worse with Emma around, I can't be the joyful mother I want to be. I tell her I'm in pain and that it is to do with the past and that seeing you always stirs something up in me and that I have to work my way through it and do my best in not putting it on her. I do put it on her so sometimes — am sharper, sterner, less playful, impatient.

Panic keeps rising in my body. I breathe into it — now. I cannot stop the pain. I feel bad about that too. I've been like this for days, it feels like a failure of some kind. Is it? I should be stronger than this. I should be more able to work my way through the self to reach the love inside. But I don't, it feels that I can't. Barry, do I have to go through all this to get clear or is it a perverse indulgence of the self again continuing the old up and down existence without getting anywhere?

What is the best thing to do when I feel this way — to get up and 'get myself out of it' or to sit and do nothing?

Evening. . .

I keep wanting to just 'collapse', to give up. It takes me enormous effort to do anything at all, yet I keep making that effort. Today I questioned it a lot. It seemed before that I had to, that it was wrong to let myself go into the pain; that I had to keep bringing myself back to function somehow in the reality of going on living with the pain in check. Yet I could actually arrange it so I could just stay in bed all day if I wanted to. Today I found myself asking myself a few times — why do I go on doing things when it is so hard to do them? — not that I do a lot but even simple things are a huge effort. What can you say — is it okay to just sink into this state of pain and tiredness? I kept wanting to do so, almost like I want just to fall back in my chair. Or is that masochism and perversity? Which bit is the self — the one that overcomes the tiredness and pain and struggles on or the bit that wants to collapse? I find the struggle really tiring. I want to let the pain drown me and not resist any more. I am extremely tired, not physically, it's another sort of tiredness.

I get so irritable and impatient and often quite angry again and I can't hold it down. It's amazing; all the techniques that have worked before don't work any more. I nag Emma and Paul and in my head there is much negative thinking. I find myself seeing what I do when I do it but not being able to stop it. Much pain goes with it. I do apologise often to Emma and explain as well as I can that it's an old pain coming up. I say things that my mother used to say, in much the same way as her. And it feels awful and then I feel the pain I think Emma feels because of it. Of course it must be my own pain somehow. I explode in a temper for small things. Oh dear. I am going on.

Paul says I'm not as bad as I feel I am and he doesn't really feel that I put much on him even though he sees my pain and struggle. He is doing well. I see a big change in him. His eyes are clearer and he is more still in the way he looks at me and altogether more in his body. He is somehow more clear and straight in the way he speaks. It's like he has more depth to him. More presence. I am pleased to see that. And he is very friendly, warm, supporting to me. He was that before but now it feels as though it's coming from a deeper place.

I do not make love with him yet, I want to see him master the sexuality in him first. After talking to you at the seminar I felt free of the pain about it and returned home very easy and feeling good. I somehow separated myself from Paul inside, that is, I stopped trying to change him, stopped the expectations and the effort and the pain coming from that.

I decided it was now up to Paul to do it or not do it and up to me to stay or not stay. I had a clear talk with him about it and I felt willing to stay and work on other things and see what came of it all, day by day. I stopped anxiously watching him and frequently asking him how he got on and trying not to create opportunities etc. I sort of went on with my own life doing my best and leaving his life up to him, still spending all our time together and talking about what goes on. It was an inside thing — and still is.

I felt I was open to man and love and it didn't matter whether it was Paul or some other body: life would bring it when it was right. It also somehow felt right to support Paul when he asked me to (that is, not pushing anything on him), in his attempt to overcome sex if that is what he really wanted.

After all I spent years in the past exciting men, in my pain and lack of love and understanding. It seems only fair that life now faces me with a sexual man and that I do some work on getting sex out of him, when really I put it into him anyway, or supported that side of him. Yes he looks good. More grown up somehow, more serene. And we really do live the way you talk — we don't let one another get away with undertones, words, moods etc or harbour any grudges. Always get things out into the open. Take time for one another. Listen.

Love from

Rosamond

Rosamond

Yes, you are right, the pain, the shame; the 'loveless monster' is your sexual past — the excitement/emotion of it — trying to re-incarnate. It wants to take over your body, to repossess it like in the old days. You, the woman, have moved on. But the past hasn't, can't. So, rising out of the subconscious where it resides in every body, it tries to regain the upper hand. You will not give it what it wants. You have purified your self by living the divine life as best you could these last two or three years. It will trouble you, as you have described. But it cannot win. It is doomed.

Nonetheless, the purer you become the harder it fights. It is it that is desperate, despairing, not you. But you can't help but identify with it when it is there because after all it is your self. And the justice of life is that I must face my self, the ignorance that I have been, and so prevent it from re-incarnating and making someone else's life a misery — usually my partner's or closest loved one's life.

We are very pleased to share our ignorance and selfishness. But not so keen to give them our love.

Your letter is a very fine exposition of what woman (and

man in his own way) has to go through in re-aligning the self, the past, to the present or presence of truth and love which is natural to every body, male and female.

Sex is the most powerful force in the world. And every man and woman's problems can be traced back to it. When sex (self) is faced rightly as you are doing it eventually loses its force — and returns to the power of love.

❖

Hello Barry

I think at last I got to a point where I can write to you about what is really going on within and without me.

I have written you some ten unposted letters already, but I always felt they were not somehow real, truthful. I can see that now more clearly, for I was writing what had happened in my life lately — and always without, outside of me. Now I suddenly can see how afraid I am about what is inside of myself, all that unhappiness.

I had had all the time one man around me, just for myself to feel I'm not left over or lonely. We didn't make love any more. Also I know now that by wanting me sexually, he gave me many opportunities not to see the truth of myself and sex etc. Now I have said to him I won't see him for a while and it's like curtains have been taken away from in front of my eyes! I have been afraid to see how much I have men's way of thinking inside of me. How much I have always been trying to please them in a sexual way — not by going to bed with them but by keeping 'sexy' clothes or flirting with almost every man. This has always been very subtle, that's why I could not see it before, at least not this clearly.

Also since I was a teenager, I have masturbated quite a lot; for I was kind of thinking it's better than being with men. I know it comes also from my parents — they didn't like each other at all, never touched or kissed; they even slept in different beds since I was born. So love was something out of place for me. Because of that the kind of men I've had were usually very cool with their feelings and always 'hooked' on something either alcohol or drugs or sex or 'getting' other women. And usually all of those things at the same time.

I feel that I have progressed with this a lot. I met a man last winter but I told him about you and said I wouldn't go to bed with him before he put his life right and started to listen to your tapes etc. He got afraid of me and said at last — after three months of being together a lot (just walking around and talking and sometimes kissing) — that he can't do this, he's not ready yet. So I told him I wouldn't see him any more. And we have not seen each other since that day.

I had never felt like that before and I know I found love with him even though he couldn't take it then!

Now I have no men around to tell me that I'm pretty or sexy. It feels good and sometimes I can feel how all this sexuality is rising inside of me. I try to be still and focus on that feeling but — like you wrote in 'Only Fear Dies' — it is very powerful and really doesn't want me to see it.

I have started having more and more sexual dreams, but I'm not having any want for sex or love-making while I am awake. I don't feel lonely or unhappy in Me! It was quite easy to tell those two men I wouldn't see them because I could keep the emotions out of that situation, even when they tried to make me emotional.

Now I just feel I have a huge work with this sexuality in me. For I can see that I still flirt with men, somehow. I haven't found a way to be without this old habit. I'm quite confused nowadays with men. Especially with those who have been with you, and can see 'my self', the sexuality. However, I try not to act like before.

I really can understand, I must be still more and more and keep the feeling that rises up in focus. That's the way.

I think I'm just a little impatient with this. I feel so ignorant — no, that's my self — yes. I can just see it so well. The other women I know, who listen to you and read you and have been in your seminars, seem not to have these kind of 'problems' at all. They seem so strong in themselves. They all have a man to live with and to 'go through' together.

I also just want to tell you that the life without, external life, has become very beautiful and peaceful. I found a little house outside the city. This is in the countryside with many forests and animals around me.

Also I stopped listening to music or the radio. Here I can listen to birds and wind in the trees, or your tapes. Television I never had before and newspapers I have never liked — but read anyway sometimes. Now I haven't read news for many months already!

So my life has changed from a very 'normal' city life with many friends and events to a peaceful and harmonious one.

I must really thank you Barry for getting my life right, joyous and earthy!

I love to hear your tapes and to read your books even though my mind tries to stop me all the time.

Thank you very very much Barry.

Pia

Pia

I'd just like to say that although you 'have no men around to tell you that you're pretty or sexy', this man here tells you, after reading your very fine letter, that you are a beautiful woman, that is, you love truth, beauty and principle and are endeavouring to live to those inner precepts. And I'd say you're living it with considerable success.

Things, meaning emotions and circumstances, keep constantly changing. But I sense in you, through your letter, a deeper and more real stream of consciousness that you have connected with. This stream is your love of truth, what I would also call your love of God, the Most High, the unknown, the principle.

Do not be seduced by your feelings. Continue to stick to what you know is right. Be well.

❖

Woman has to be strong enough in her resolve to be love to make man face her in honesty and truth

Dear Barry

First I like to thank you for being with us. I enjoy listening to your tapes, reading your books and being with you. Still there is a question which keeps coming up because my boyfriend is going to bed with other women. And while I am trying to keep watching my emotions I get the idea he is stimulating his by going out and having sex. (He says he wants to stop his sexual behaviour.)

Urma

Urma

It is your life, no one else's. So what do you want — or better still what don't you want in your life? Do you want your man to be going to bed with other women? If not, leave him. Otherwise, you will be unhappy, the other women will be unhappy and he will continue to be restless and unhappy.

Why are you watching your emotions while he's doing this? Who told you to do that — he? If so, is he a sannyasin? I'll tell you now what your emotions are at that time and always will be — deeply disturbed.

The reason is you can perceive no purpose in what he is doing; he is only serving his self. If there was purpose in his action the other women would be becoming freer and freer of unhappiness; you would be becoming less and less emotional (unhappy) because in your deepest place you would know he was a man of love bringing more love into the world; and he would be free of unhappiness as part of the purpose of his love and loving.

❖

Dear Barry

How wonderful it is that you are on the earth speaking the love and living truth you are. I honour the wisdom you speak, the difference it makes in my life and your great service.

I have had a few questions arising in me over the last months, have endeavoured to come to my own resolutions and have not yet totally succeeded.

About seven or eight months ago I had a chance to really look at my jealousy and attachment.

My partner decided to follow up an attraction that he had for another woman, to spend time with her and then after a few months, to make love with her. He said he had no excitement in the union. This was all with my full knowledge. I did not 'want' him to make love with her and yet had some idea that I 'should' be able to let go of my attachment; that I should be able to let him love and be loved by someone else and that it should help free me of my jealousy. What actually occurred for me were large swings between numbness and full denial of my feelings, to a feeling of my heart literally being torn in two, or, eventually intense rage and a sense of 'this just cannot be happening' (like one can feel at hearing the unbearable) and hatred as I have never allowed myself to experience.

At the beginning it was easier because he seemed to 'love me enough' but our relationship worsened and I became more emotional and he more distant and unpleasant. I lived with the words 'either she goes or I go' in my head but did not say them. I was attached and unwilling to lose him and I was endeavouring to work with my jealousy.

Finally, having been haunted by this issue, I reached a very clear place in that I actually did not mind which way it went but I wanted a monogamous, committed relationship. He had some insight into what he had been up to and decided to commit totally to a monogamous relationship and has been in total integrity ever since.

I still find that it is difficult for me if he has any contact with her (she is part of our local community). I also find things which trigger old feelings in me (like sitting having tea alone with the kids at night) seem to keep arising.

I am not sure where to draw the line between indulgence of suffering and denial! It is definitely not a complete issue for me and I am not sure where to go with it now. I have difficulty with my partner being intimate with any woman, and he also has difficulty in me being intimate with other men. I often hold myself back completely with men and can feel threatened by other women.

How to tame the great green-eyed monster?

If I 'think' of them together it makes me feel sick beyond all reason as if someone had just told me of some shocking, shocking event.

I had never realised how emotional I am!

The second issue I have arises around sex and making love. I have endeavoured to follow your teaching for quite a few years now and vacillate between the 'discipline' of making love, in which there is a great sense of rightness in me, and a relief from the vulgarity and violence of sex, to feeling that I am actually denying my nature which is also passionate, wild and sexual. My partner believes sex to be a natural part of being alive. He sees no wrong in occasionally looking at Playboy, or masturbating and not 'denying' his sexual nature. I see that the sex in the world upsets me. I hide from the truth of man and the truth of myself. Somehow now I must find my own truth within this. I have also used your teaching in the past to hide in, to not deal with the way things are; to be ever so pure and yet not look at my own beauty and ugliness. I am not clear in which direction to go with it. I swing so between the two places.

The last issue arises out of my latest pregnancy. I have a want to branch out beyond motherhood, to serve the wider community in other ways and to come and attend your seminars. I can feel the joy and bliss of being pregnant again and also frustration at the surrender. I seem to have set my life up in a pushing/pulling kind of a way.

I would be very grateful to have any comments on these situations.

Thank you again, Barry, for everything you are and the loving your presence has brought and continues to bring into my life.

Suzanne

Suzanne

I know you have endeavoured to apply my teaching as you have seen it to be the truth of your own experience. You write to me with a couple of problems or questions, so now I must remind you of a fundamental of my teaching which neither you nor your partner are heeding. He conveniently overlooks it and justifies his own teaching which then leads to the problems besetting you. And you perpetuate your unhappiness by overlooking my teaching and letting him get away with his.

There is no doubt that sex, the interaction as love between two bodies, is a natural part of being alive, as your partner says. But occasionally looking at Playboy and masturbating is not a natural part of being alive; nor is it part of love's sexual nature. It is man-made — or mind-made — selfish sex, and this denial of love will always make woman emotional because she subconsciously knows — as you should certainly know — that it is corruption.

The obvious proof of this is that looking at Playboy excites the imagination in which there is only one body, that of the looker; and in masturbating there is again only one body and some phantom image of another. The man throws a red herring (which many men will repeat) by saying he sees no wrong in 'not denying' his sexual nature in those ways. What he needs to do is to deny his sexual self and not smokescreen his actions by calling his sexual self his sexual nature.

His dishonesty, and yours, in not facing it and dealing with it, even if he leaves you, is behind your jealousy. How can you truly love a man who prefers phantoms to you? All jealousy is due to the frustration of trying to love someone who does not love you enough. Jealousy is an effort of the mind and emotions to fill the break in what should be the ring of love. And of course the fear, or attachment of facing the dishonesty that he does not love you enough, keeps you bound to a broken or flawed ring. When I man truly love a woman, that woman cannot be jealous of another woman whom I love. It is impossible.

It is also possible that your frequent pregnancies are a compensation for your inability to expose the ring of love between you and the men you love. You subconsciously feel a baby will fill the gap. But it doesn't. And it never will. Nonetheless I know it is good that you are pregnant and I would in no way have you in any doubt about that. You are a good woman and I know you will do your best with the child, as you always have endeavoured. It's just time that you have to face the truth of the woman that you are and stop compromising with man's selfish teaching of love, which never fails to reveal itself to woman in her right mind as self indulgence. It's not your jealousy you have to overcome; it is your fear of losing him.

❖

Dear Barry

As I have told you before, since I have been endeavouring in earnest to live the divine life according to the truth I hear in your teaching, there have been profound changes in the circumstances of my life. I am still surprised at how simple the solutions are if I am truly honest to the situation. There is, at present, however, one area of myself causing me some confusion which I am finally moved to ask you about as I am not certain that my understanding is a true one. Am I right in feeling that it is the hardest thing for a woman to detach from the impulse towards personalising her love? This is my experience.

I am as present as I can see how to be with my lover; I face him as straightly as I can, we speak of love and truth and rarely of the past. I am taking responsibility to rid myself of moods and emotions of which only jealousy and self-comparison assert themselves with any force now (and even those, thank God, are lessening immeasurably). And yet personal attachment still creeps in. I am at a loss as to how to stop this happening. My feeling is that attachment will keep occurring but that I will, as has been glimpsed in my experience, be able to reduce sufficient self in me so that I can feel love or nothing even when my heart is being broken.

A few months ago, out of the blue, a couple of situations arose which did indeed succeed in breaking my heart. First, my lover declared he could no longer feel his love and had to leave. And then he announced his desire of other women of which, astonishingly to me now, I had blinded myself to and had not even suspected. In both cases I felt destroyed yet was able to find sufficient presence both times to say without bitterness or anger that if that was the truth he must then leave me. Deep down I knew my suffering was a result of the attachment I had allowed to creep in. Without your teaching I would not have faced this situation with such clarity. As it was, Mike was able to surrender to some self, stay facing me and is now doing his very best for love.

What still troubles me, however, is that I have done and continue to do my best to stay true to love and yet I still must be personalising my love along the way. I know this when I feel the occasional pang of jealousy, which I suppose is why I am stung so to keep me alert to the self I still carry within me. I acknowledge the suffering I have caused myself with past lovers through indulging painful imaginings fuelled by betrayal, but I no longer allow this which is a relief. Is it simply that I am impatient and expecting to be rid of my suffering self too quickly?

Does my surrender to love mean a willingness to keep having my heart broken of attachments which ultimately I can't stop occurring to some (though lesser as my self lessens) degree? Or might I ultimately transcend all attachment? I feel that the former is true and if I can be the stillness in me knowing what I am doing, I will stay conscious in love and not be lost in notions of love and suffering. Is there anything more I can do which I am not doing? I cannot see what else to do other than be even more honest in how I live my life now and not attach myself to an idea that eventually I could reach a state of being where I am freed of personal love, jealousy and self-comparison altogether. Perhaps I have already answered my question.

Thank you for your teaching.

Gail

Gail

Events will have moved on for you since you wrote to me a few months ago. And I have been abroad a couple of times since then. Because you are so earnest I will endeavour to address the main difficulty you raise in your letter.

The breaking of the heart is simply the breaking of attachment to the notions of love. When the heart is pure — purified of attachment — there is no more suffering, no more attachment. This, as you know, is easier said than done. But done it must be for there is no other immediate purpose to life than to purify the heart of its attachments and suffering, which finally means its attachment to suffering.

Life must be seen and lived as it is. No man can undertake to love only you. He may love only you but he cannot undertake or promise to do that. Woman's notion (and his own at the time) is that he can. But he can't. When a man undertakes or promises this, he is satisfying the expectations or notions of love of the woman. And he becomes subconsciously frustrated. This frustration is what causes his restlessness, anger and moods (in the first instance). This is not to defend man's inability to love the woman he is with but just to say how it is. The fact is that when he is tied to one woman by her expectations or his fear of her emotional reactions, he cannot be the man he is, that is, the passionate, attentive and responsive man she knew him to be when they first met. Then he was tied to no woman and his abandoned, exciting and ardent way of wooing and loving her was the natural result of his freedom and attraction to her. As soon as he begins to realise he is no longer free the rot, the awareness of the collar, sets in. This is the case in every man unless, as I say, he does not feel restricted by the woman's notions and expectations of what he should be. Man must be free to love, to love you, as you love to be loved.

Am I condoning man's sexual restlessness? Of course not. Man can only be free when he is fearless; when he is not afraid of woman, when he is not afraid to love her up to the hilt, all the way. And yet, at the same time not to abide her emotional notions and dreams of how he should be, which destroy the man in him for himself and the man in him for her. Both lose when man is afraid. And that is what has happened to the love of man and woman on earth.

Man today is unfit for freedom. He wants the freedom without giving up his fear. And that is ignoble. He wants to love other women while being cowed by the woman he is with, terrified of what she will say or emotionally do to him, hiding his sexuality in masturbatory fantasies or illicit affairs. He is unable to face woman and love her as a real man, love her as he knows love is and not bow to her acquired selfish, possessive and jealous notions of what it is to love man. In his fearlessness he must absolve her dream so that she can be fulfilled in real love which she has lost the knowledge of. She has become women instead of Woman, a collection of personal impressions of love which are simply the opposite of love or the attempt to escape from the hurts and pains she has known from man's cowardly love in the past. She wants to possess him for herself alone to selfishly heal the aches of her broken, bruised and disillusioned hearts. In her jealousy, her fiendish emotional holding on to him and flagellating of him, she tries to get — and in getting she loses everything that every woman longs for: the real love of real man. In conquering him she is vanquished. He is a wimp. She is unhappy. He is unhappy. And together they try unsuccessfully to make the best of it with a nice home, some kids and lots of plans for the future. Or the man runs, dipping in to many women in his fear of ever loving enough to be the master of love that he truly is.

So what is to be done?

To return man and woman to love without fear or selfishness is a process. It was a process of forgetfulness and ignorance which got them into the sorry state they are in today; and so it is a process for them to return to the beginning again. A process has stages. And the first stage is for woman to be in command of love and not to demand love. She has to be strong enough in her resolve to be love (love is what she is), to make man who says he loves her face her in honesty and truth. To do this she must give up her attachment to suffering, to the broken hearts and hurts of the past. She must put love which is courageous before her self which is her pain. Crucially, she must not make love to the man unless he is facing her in honesty and truth. She must deny him his most urgent need to escape. At the same time she must be loving and giving.

If the man threatens to leave her, she must tell him never to threaten her again in that way, and if he intends to, to go now, this moment. She must not give in to her weeping heart, that organ of past ignorance and attachment which may feel as though it is about to break. She must be true to what she is doing, to what she is being; be true to love and not true to her past self. She must die for love.

This will make her woman enough. She may lose that man, and others. But it is better that one woman on this earth realises the power that is Woman, on behalf of love, than a million women indulge a dishonest man through giving in to the force of his sexual manipulation.

Only when a woman is woman enough to actually die for love in this way, can a fearless man come to her and teach her the way out of her emotional misconceptions, and return her to the living love she is in essence. She will then learn and finally know the secret of the term making love or to make love.

Making love or to make love is, for her, simply to make woman woman. And for man, if he is man enough to make woman, he then is already made, is already here.

I am more real within you than without

❖

Dear Barry

I would like to thank you for the last series of lectures you gave. I found them most inspiring and, as ever, they deepened and prolonged my ability to embody.

I had two quite powerful experiences during these lectures that I would like to feed back to you. The first came one evening when you were talking about the female principle. I was listening from a deep sense of what seemed in retrospect, 'gender-less being', when suddenly I made a 'lateral shift' in consciousness, and clicked into pure female principle. Nothing male, nothing worldly to distort or contaminate it, but very very familiar, and like coming home.

The second experience came as you were taking us consciously into the unconscious for the first time. The exercise felt very familiar to me, due to two decades of meditation practice, yet there was something about it that was also very different. As you announced what we were going to do, my whole being exulted energetically with a resounding 'Yes!'(unvoiced). This was followed by a sense of overwhelming relief and the feeling of having received healing which lasted for several days afterwards.

Strange and simplistic as it may sound, at the time I felt as if you had recognised and validated publicly my deepest, truest, most secret inner being. Something I have consciously kept hidden from the world since I was a child. And with it came a feeling of having returned more fully to my original nature.

I feel very fortunate and grateful to have met you. You are in deed the spiritual master: the living example of the living truth, that my heart has yearned for, for so long; though not believing it was possible, in these barren times, to meet such a one as you — and yet, here you are, now, within me. Thank you Barry.

Stephanie

Stephanie

It is clear that you have made more profound and meaningful contact with your deepest secret place that you have always known. The law of existence is that the potential within — the limitless place of love/knowledge in every body — can only be realised through the triggering or mirroring of external events and contacts. Thus, experience is the only way to self-realisation and the liberation of being. But experience itself is not enough. There must be a depth of reflection within, paralleling, to be effective, the depth of reflection of the various cosmic bodies without. For instance, if the person's inner reflection is only equal to the shallow distance of worldly or materialistic considerations without, there will be little realisation of their potential. But if the inner reflection is equal to the outer spatial depth of the planetary orbs, the realisation will be much more profound and fulfilling. If the reflection should reach solar depth the love and knowledge implicit in the presence is great — for it is then of stellar quality. And so the parallel continues, out to the constellations etc for there is no end or limit to the depth of consciousness represented by the heavens. This is the true origin of the aphorism 'as within, so without'. You will perceive here the meaning of cosmic consciousness.

The depth of reflection within is determined by the

individual's capacity and ability to suffer rightly — for only pain digs out ignorance. Love's job and pleasure is to fill all such holes. And since love is the only true medium of communication — the depth of selflessness or right suffering to surrender to love or the Most High becomes the depth of inner and outer reflection and perception. 'As I am is how it is.'

You have drawn the mirror that I am to you and that, together with your own depth of reflection, has triggered the perceptions and insights described in your letter. It is true, I am more real within you than without.

❖

Dear Barry Long, beloved Guru

I am so grateful to you for this feeling that you have restored in me — at the very core of me — by your love. It is a very strong thing and it is there all the time, almost all the time and it really is sort of completely sufficient.

You said (in your leaflet) 'come to me with your fear and I'll expose its roots' and that is exactly what you have done for me. But now it transpires: to drop the fear I have to drop illusions which I had. It seems I am beginning to understand that love can only be impersonal, that what I took to be love was just partial tolerance, limited and conditional acceptance. But what a terrible responsibility, the aloneness of it and the self-discipline required. I am struggling with it and it manifests outside of me. But of course I know this is what I have been looking for as long as I can remember.

I love you. I love you. I love you.

Laura

Laura

Yes, you have indeed received the love that is impersonal, the love behind the intimacy of any body. Your words show that — that you are now true to love. This you will remain — for it is the core of you — although the grins and growls of circumstance will try to shake you.

Know that I know what you are giving within you.

[Six weeks later she wrote again.]

Dear Barry Long, beloved Master

Meeting you has made a deep impression on me and the impact of it on my daily life is still enormous. Most of all it made me realise how terribly dishonest I was/am, and how dishonest my relationships were. That I was doing so many things with a certain purpose instead of really wanting to do them. The worst of course, was my dishonesty towards my partner. I like him, oh definitely, but most of all I wanted to keep him attached to me to help me raise the children, for you see, I had been trying to raise them alone but that didn't work out so well. I couldn't really take the responsibility. Now I am stronger it seems. And anyway, shedding some of the dishonesty has greatly helped the relationship from my point of view at least.

A big problem that I have with shedding my past is that I am so, well to be honest, so proud of it. All those dangers overcome, all those wounds healed, all those shoddy experiences left behind and look at me now. It is as if I need the contrast, you see, to be something. It is quite obvious. And I can still picture you answering to this, 'be still'. So I'll get back at stilling myself again but I did have this great urge to gush out words to you. I feel so much love. I just have to think the word 'guru' and I feel my whole body respond. But perhaps this is not a right thing to do.

But I love you, that's one thing I'm not in doubt about.

Laura

Laura

The thing that you love, of course, is the unspeakable sweetness in your body, the Lord, your most intimate energetic essence — and I, this consciousness in man in the world, reflect it to you. It is the way of things that the essential love within can only be realised through an external trigger or reflection. In the realm of likes and dislikes — the ordinary superficial world — this triggering is going on continuously as we like that car, that dress, that person but dislike this one and this one and this one. So continues the habitual world where likes — even amid our families — are so often mistaken for love. You have begun stepping out of that world by looking into a subjective mirror — my being — instead of into the normally prized and deluding objective ones. For contrary to what the scientists and the world say, the truth and love are subjective. What is objective is simply the fact — and the fact is not the truth. The fact is only true for now. But as you know love is forever, meaning now which never ends. Is that the truth of your love Laura?

❖

Dear Barry Long

Would you like to make love with me? I long to. I write to you because there is a part in me, a yes, I like to enjoy life, and I receive you as so beautiful. Thank you.
In love

Tessa

Tessa

The intense feeling of your love of me, and my beauty, is your love of God (or the Lord) within, and the beauty of that within. I have become a focus for you outside through which you reduce your love down to a searing point that burns (away the matter, the problem) within.

I know this is of little comfort while you are reducing your self, or being reduced, like this. But it is all I can do. I know your beauty and your truth and you do not complain. I also know your love.

But no matter what our short lives, and our longer days, tell us, our existence — the purpose of it — is to become pure in God. Not all, not many, are able to know this consciously. To be conscious of the purpose while we are afflicted (by love or pain) shows that we are well advanced in the process. This you are, dear Tessa. Love loves thee.

I'm counting on you

How many women, Barry Long, how many are totally and utterly free?

My life is in ruins. I have been spat on, humiliated, violated and emotionally raped by man. Suppressed, forced to do, be, act, talk, work, etc by someone else, always their words.

There is not one woman I know who is free and totally herself. That's why she knits and makes wall hangings.

There are many women changing their lifestyles and activities. They read Barry Long and think they have attained their love. They only take Barry Long on board and think this other method is it. How many women do you know who do not become what Barry Long wants? — eventually?

Don't point me to your tapes. I've got them all. If this is it why isn't the world full of beautiful, joyful love-filled people?

Holly

'How many women, Barry Long, how many are totally and utterly free?'

There's only one who can do it and be it, Holly Harrison, only one — and I'm counting on you.

Get on with it.

Woman must never be just a mother — she is always a lover

❖

Dear Barry Long

I want to write to you about me and Jonathan, my almost five year old son. In a seminar I told you that I felt often disturbed in my relationship with him, not knowing what was the 'right' thing to do; feeling I had to make lots of little decisions all day, every day and feeling divided. You told me to follow my feelings and that I knew what to do.

I still feel the disturbance in bringing up my son although some things have cleared. I seem to have followed my feelings all along but often feel great uncertainty and doubt about the things I do or don't do. And with some things I now feel I definitely made lots of mistakes.

For example, I was very much in favour of breastfeeding him and felt it was good for him as well as enjoyable to us both. I fed him on demand and he never took to food until he was two years old. Even then it was me insisting on feeding him less. I still breastfeed him at night before he goes to sleep but reading your books and listening to you makes me wonder now — is the breast just another outside thing that directs his attention and energy outside of himself? Have I done him a disservice by getting him attached to breastfeeding? I used to think if he had his fill of everything he'd be okay with himself without having to carry around the unfulfilled wanting feelings. Also it seemed to me such a beautiful time spent together, a lovely way to end the day for both of us.

Other doubts are now emerging. I sleep with Jonathan. All three of us used to sleep together. Then we felt Simon and me were not sleeping well enough, especially Simon as he had to go to work every morning. So now he sleeps in the room next door. We both lie down with Jonathan in the evening until he goes to sleep. Do I deprive him of enjoying himself on his own? I remember you mentioning in 'Only Fear Dies' how a baby lies there gurgling with the joy of life and how parents and others take him out of himself, draw his attention on to things and make him dependent on cuddles. I've cuddled Jonathan a lot. Still do! And so far he's always gone to sleep in my arms drinking milk.

Of course the world around me in the form of doctors, parents, relatives and so on has always criticised these things but I don't trust anybody in what they say. Alas I don't trust myself either! I feel quite alone yet without the knowledge of how to do rightly. I keep looking around for someone to help me, yet you say we all know inside but I look inside and find no answers. I do the best I can — as you say we all do — yet it doesn't seem enough.

With love

Chloe

Chloe

I've received your letter and will do my best to answer some main points but I can't really tell you how to bring up your child. You have to know what you are doing. And that means not following your feelings. This may lead to some confusion to begin with as the mind speculates. But if you listen in stillness you'll get the point. Feelings are likes and dislikes and they are not reliable. What you feel is right today you'll be unsure of tomorrow because the emotions, like a pendulum, get their strength of quasi-stability from swinging backwards and forwards.

The constant feeling underneath the feelings is the feeling of wellbeing that I constantly refer to in my teaching. This is always there and the practice is as often as possible to connect with it and be it. This constant feeling (all other feelings are inconstant) transforms into knowledge. It is feelings that know and do not know and it is the feeling that is knowledge, which is equilibrium or steadiness. This feeling then is clarity. And in clarity I know what I am doing.

About breastfeeding I cannot tell you what is right. You know for yourself and your child, the extension of yourself. But this must be from knowledge, not from feelings which your confusion shows are inconstant and unreliable. I suggest that a child should be taken off the breast by at most 12 months, if not before. It should be done by the mother having the knowledge of what is right, and by not necessarily following books or others' opinions.

It may be time to try something different, most babies (like ourselves) having turned into such horrible messes. If you get the life right between man and woman then perhaps the child will turn out right. Milk is love in substance and that's for the baby. The love of the breast is to nourish man and the psychic or immortal love between the man and woman. The way things are everybody seems to consider the baby's need of love and not the man's. The first is filling a necessary animal need. The second is the recognition of sustaining love or power beyond the animalistic needs.

The most important thing on earth is the love between the mother and father of the child. This alone will change things including the baby when he or she grows up. Love of the child must be secondary or everyone in the family unit will become discontented and unhappy. The breasts in the first instance are for the child until solid and appropriate substitute liquids can be taken. That is love. The breasts are then for the man to receive through them the nourishment of love from the woman. Man is really a child and without this nourishment of love he becomes weak in the sense of hard and unloving. If a woman's breast makes a child healthy it does no less for her man.

While you have breastfed Jonathan for so many years it is doubtful that your man will have received much of this nourishment. He will have been starved. You will have put the child well before your joint love. He will inevitably become frustrated and discontented and this will reflect in your life together. It may drive him to sleep in the other room, which you say has already happened, although the reasons for this will be quite rational. Also, your practice in sleeping with the child will have alienated your man.

You had better get it right as soon as you can. Put first things first. Do what you do because you know why you are doing it and stop following your feelings.

One final word and I want you to read this whenever you read some other part of this letter. You must not be guilty about anything you have done with Jonathan or Simon. Guilt is one of the feelings of likes and dislikes and is destructive of love. Do what is right now from your own knowledge without any reference to the past. You must live and operate from that place as much as possible. That is love.

❖

Dear Barry

May I write to you again? I would appreciate it if you would grant me your response to some things that bother me. Love is not the problem: Cliff and I are doing fine. Living together is not happening yet but I am not impatient.

My children are pulling away from me towards their father. I am not unhappy about their absence in the house, I do not miss them when they aren't there (and I do enjoy their presence when they are) but I am worrying whether I am to blame in some respect.

At the moment the father and I are sharing childcare; half of the week they are at his house, half at mine. We don't live far apart so the arrangement is quite easy in practice. He has a new woman and she is nice to the kids. At first the boy had problems with her but these are overcome now. Actually I seem to have helped there. For when he started to complain about her to me and said that he didn't love her, I asked him, 'Do you love me?'

'Yes', he said. I said, 'If you love one woman, you can love other women too'. He quickly cottoned on to that idea and said, 'That's just like when you are a member of the main library, you can have books from other libraries as well'. I said, 'Exactly'.

That seemed to help. At the other house people were working on the problem too. Until that time, the kids were at their father's two days and with me five; from then on they expressed the wish to stay on at the father's place longer and the half-half arrangement was made.

Now they are saying they want to be with him more, again. For instance, five days with him, two with me. They asked me to talk to the father about this and I did.

Nothing has been decided yet but I feel so strange about all this, so double. On the one hand it is easy for me; I have my work which I can't squeeze into half a week and so less childcare means more time and more ease in the work area. Also, even though Cliff loves the kids and they love him (this is definitely the case, they get on really well now), he also welcomes the idea of more time for the two of us.

But on the other hand it worries me that I might be an inadequate mother. I couldn't resist asking the boy why he preferred his father's house and he said, 'Because we get to school earlier when he takes us and because he gives us meat to eat'. Both the father and his woman live on welfare so they have much more time and attention for the children than I do. I do feel that I do my best but I must admit that I often fail in being a responsible and loving parent. This causes a nagging doubt. Also I am probably simply jealous.

Actually I don't even know what exactly is the question to you here for I can't ask you whether I am good enough as a mother; I should know myself, shouldn't I? But there is an emotion in this situation that I cannot quite handle because it is hard to identify.

Would you please comment?

Hannah

Hannah

You cannot be a good mother and a good lover. The truer you become or are as woman, the more you will perceive and be aware of the compromise. Compromise — being attached to two things and thinking you can get away with it — is the way of the world. And it works there, providing the swinging pendulum between like and dislikes, between this and that, driving the person by force of conflict and division to live and accept as natural the life of being happy today and unhappy tomorrow. The problematical way is the way of the world and its root is compromise.

Now about the children and you. The emotion is the notion of mother. It's trying to be what you are not. You are mother as much as you are mother: caring, loving, responsible. But you can only be at any moment what you are. You are also lover (to Cliff) and a working woman. You can be all three. As long as when you are one you don't try or think you should be being the other. That's relationship. One blends into the other — as emotional division. And you are neither one nor the other. Love the children with your wisdom and straightness. The children have their simple, uncomplicated (uncompromising) reasons for preferring to be with their father for now, as the boy so beautifully expressed it, 'We get to school earlier when he takes us and he gives us meat to eat'. And the husband's woman (by the grace of love) is good to them — as Cliff is. This is all coming from Thee, the centre of it all. It is all pretty good, really, isn't it? It's just the mind wanting to be all things at once — when it itself is not even one thing, one resolution, for long.

Be what you are now — and don't try to mindfully impose it on what you were yesterday. Give up, let go. But when you are that — whatever it is — be it, do it. Get rid of the fuzzy edges, the wanting to be two things. Each in its moment as long as it lasts. Then the next. It can and does change in minutes. I'm working at my desk. I'm all that. The boy comes in and asks a question. I'm now mother.

I'm all that — mother, attentive, fully listening to what he has to say without one thought about what I was working on or doing before. I answer him. If I see his need is not great, I say in truth and without impatience: 'I am working. I will be finished within an hour. That's how it must be. Then I will be with you or attend to what you need'. Back to the job. No thought about the boy. Then, as you said, give him what you said you would. Explain about being responsible for what you are, for what you are doing, being. He will hear you — the good practical sense of it. And as he grows he will love you for it — and always return to talk and be with his wise and loving mother who seemed to be able to be all things. I am what I am.

Dear Barry

My daughter Arabella left today. She has either disposed of or taken with her everything she owns. She has, as you say, thrown herself open to the Law of life.

Her bedroom is almost as though she never existed and I am suffering — the baby in my womb is dying, and I try to contain the pain as you teach. I try not to think but just to be with it. Each time the emotion starts to rise I keep it down in my belly and try to be still, but I know there is a lot of pain there, I can feel the link with all the other pains — death of mother, brother, other loved ones as well as relationships.

There is much love in me and I thank you for helping me to find it again.

I gave Arabella my blessing before she left and I know that the lovely maturing young lady that she is can face whatever there is to face, but I do so want to be there if needed. But of course I am no longer needed, and that's how it should be.

Something I notice Barry, when I face emotional pain, often I have a hot flush — I am going through the menopause — I feel somehow that this is just one of the tricks that my brain uses — 'look at what this is doing to you' — it seems to say, and it soon passes when I don't dwell on it.

There doesn't seem to be any need to write any more. There is some stillness in me now.

God bless.

Love

Anne

Anne

You are a brave and wise woman. She has gone, as you say, because she must. She too must enter man's world — and know the pain, the heartbreak and joy of it. She must learn to rise above suffering — as you must — by loving man and not becoming attached to him, or his man-made world of problems. He will bring her to her knees with his burden of the world. But I am here with you, woman, to help you up by showing you the reflection of your own power. You are made for love not for attachment. And your letter shows, Anne, that although the burden of the world has attached itself to you over the years, you are detaching from it. You have found the power of woman in yourself. And you rightly call it love. It takes time to shed the burden. Do not be discouraged. Woman's love is woman's love, not man's. He must find man's love, to free himself of his own burden, his own self-inflicted world. But it is woman's time now. And I, man who bound you, am now here as my teaching, to make amends and free you. Yes, emotional pain will bring on menopausal hot flushes. That's all it is. Don't dwell on it in the brain. Love is letting go.

❖

Be open to life,
the new,
the unknown

❖

Dear Barry

I felt very positive after your last seminar. You may remember that I spoke to you because I was beginning to feel I was losing my clarity and connection with the divine life. I explained to you that I had been on my own without a partner since my divorce a year ago and felt and still feel that love is distinctly lacking from life. Now I feel that I am getting dragged down once again by the tedium and struggle of living and can't seem to be able to find the love in me, or any closeness to life. I suppose I am what the psychotherapists would term 'depressed', the only difference being that, thanks to you, over the past two years I have known the truth of life and have known great clarity at times — what you would call God consciousness. Why is it then that now I appear to be going backwards?

When I spoke to you I told you that within the space of a year I had managed to get my external life right and clear and do not have any more problems. So why am I now so confused in my internal life? I read your books and listen to your tapes over and over, but I have such a longing to meet a partner who I could share this truth with. You assured me that I would meet someone soon, and I trust it will happen one day, but I am disappointed in myself as I wanted to be able to find joy and to be free of unhappiness without depending on an 'other'. I want to be able to love impersonally but am finding it so hard. This 'down' always happens a couple of months after being with you. Somehow I don't manage to retain the powerful and positive energy I get from you and I allow myself to be dragged back to the world and experience the awfulness and meaninglessness of living. How do I get back to the God within?

It did me so much good to feel your presence and be connected with you. I'm really grateful to you for that. I went away feeling much less alone and filled with your energy. Mostly, I find it hard to connect with people and most of those around me aren't spiritually conscious, which makes me feel more alone.

I hope that this doesn't sound like a 'sad story'. I assure you I have stopped telling them! I am writing to you in earnest. Discovering you as master has completely changed my life, even if at times I feel hopeless.

Stella

Stella

You get these depressions because you need to be loved. You are buoyed after being with me because you know I truly love you, that is, my energy actually penetrates the matter of your body, the plate of mind, to your flesh which is the sweet, soft real part of you that lives off love and truth. You need to be loved physically, as you know, but also by a man who hears the truth as you do. That is true mateship.

The matter of our body, the plate of mind around the flesh, is something we have acquired as a race and developed personally to protect us from the lack of love in the world and our own subsequent feelings of vulnerability. We become 'strong', mentally strong, so that we can cope and appear to be coping. But this strength creates fear of being vulnerable, that is, anxiety about opening ourselves to love. So we dam ourselves, the natural outgoing psychic flow, and contribute to the lovelessness of the world. We then feel alone and the 'awfulness and meaningless of living', as you describe. We feel we are waiting on someone to come to love us and this in turn makes us feel we don't want to depend on an 'other', as you also describe.

The point is that you have to do it. You have to open yourself psychically to the love of man. You have to face your own enclosure and fear. You will probably feel you don't know how to do this or that it is just words and that I do not really understand your position. But I do.

You have to break through this matter, this psychological circle you have drawn around yourself. It is like, and is in fact, what in occult terms is called the guardian of the threshold or the ring-pass-not. Both mean that you are not permitted to go on to the next fulfilling stage of your life until you face and by right action, and right being, pass through the fearful guardian and the ring-pass-not. Right being you have, for I know your love and earnestness in this matter. Now it requires the action.

In occult practices there is a selfishness, a search for magical power, that makes the whole occult world a place of self-seeking disguised as spiritual practice. What you are doing, or will do if you hear me correctly, is gaining nothing for yourself. The action will be the dying to self, by the sacrifice of self, fear. You must be true to your own vulnerability. You must be vulnerable. You must be available by a psychic arms-outstretchedness to man to love you. You must stand naked in love without fear for yourself. This is a holy inner poise, a smilingness out towards the world of man.

And your protection? Your protection is your experience.

Up till now your protection has been your fear. You know from having lived as woman what you do not want. No man can force himself upon you ever again. No man can fool you with his sweet words, his gifts, his charm. For you are a woman of love, of God, the knowledge of life. You know what the love of man is. You do not expect him to be a god or an angel. You only want him to be true to love and willing to learn by your mutual interaction, as you are, to be able to talk about life and truth, to be vulnerable to his own inner reality, and to be honest so that mood, anger, avoidance, resentment, guilt and fear are gradually transcended in both. Stay with the fact not the excuse. If I am lonely in this world the fact is that I have closed myself off to love. So it is with any other negativity I entertain and indulge in myself. Selfishness is behind every negativity.

You must be willing, Stella. You have lived enough and loved enough to be this woman that you are. This way you are not dependent on the other. You are doing it, you are responsible. You know what you are doing and why you are doing it. You must make this first move inwardly and that will bring the outward manifestation of your own willingness to love.

Be joyous, as you face outward, in the knowledge that I, the love of man, am with you inside.

❖

Dear Barry

My marriage ended over twenty years ago, and since then I have not had a relationship with anyone, man or woman. I notice in my relationship with others that when people touch me physically, it is almost invariably in a somewhat aggressive manner, like being hit. I realise they may not mean to hurt and it may be only an endeavour to get closer to me or perhaps drive home a point. But it is something I dislike more than I can say. Such is my need of physical love and this careless, brusque, aggressive touch is almost my only experience in the years since my marriage ended. You have said, 'You are starved of love because you do not dare to love'. By practising your teaching, I know increasingly how fearful I am, yet also how much more conscious I am of this.

I spoke to you at a seminar and said how I longed above all for a relationship with a man but saw how on the (all too rare) occasions that I meet someone, I somehow do not encourage closeness. You responded to my raising of this issue with great kindness and encouragement and I thank you for this with all my heart. I felt from what you said or how you said it (I cannot now recall the exact words) that I was close to the possibility of a relationship and I was learning to love myself more, but this still has not materialised.

In the 'Making Love' tapes you say, 'If you are serious and earnest about loving you will eventually draw to yourself a person who will share the start of this great adventure with you'. It is four years now since I first heard those tapes and still it has not, it seems, been the divine will for me.

Jane

Jane

Regarding man, have you really in these last four years opened yourself to opportunity when he came and intimated his interest? He does not necessarily come on his white charger, you know. He who may be right for you, is often as diffident as you are, though the need of love is as pressing. You must respond to mutual attraction, encourage subtly or gently; this is to overcome the fear or shadow in you which is a form of self protection. You want but are you prepared to give? You must give. This shadow is what has kept man from you or what has made you fail to accept the opportunity when it came.

He will come again and give you another chance. Be vigilant but do not look for ideals. Your body needs to be loved. Take things or him as they are as long as you feel the attraction and he displays love or tenderness in his interchange with you.

❖

Dear Barry

Thank you for writing. I am sorry that I was unable to come to your teaching day.

When I read your letter the first time it made sense, but later when I read it it made me angry. You say I am being guided by my fate towards my 'inevitable destiny of fulfilment in love, union and passion'. But who says that is my inevitable destiny? It could be quite different couldn't it? Many people end up lonely and unloved.

I am not impatient because I am busy with teenagers to finish bringing up but I am anxious because I've waited this long (I'm 48) and I've not got it yet. I worry about getting too old. You say 'Do what you want'. I do love a man whom I have known since before I married. He is 57, still a bachelor, and when I am with him I feel I have come home, that this is where I belong, that he is the part of me that is missing — and I feel complete. Yet he obviously doesn't feel the same about me. In the context of divine love and justice, that isn't fair. Unless he wants me with him all the time as I want him, I can never be happy. So how can I do what I want? I know what I should do: completely forget him. But that is not what I want. I also feel there is no one else in the world I could feel so complete with.

That is some of the story. I wish I could resolve this.

With best wishes and sorry about the teaching day. I hope it was a successful day.

Rosemary

Rosemary

It's all a process of getting your thinking straight: you've got to see things as they are and not as you wish they were.

For instance. How can you be sorry you were unable to come to my meeting? You did what you wanted, instead. You knew what you were doing and you did it. You may be sorry for yourself (that you can't think straight therefore can't live straight) but you're not really sorry. It's a matter of putting first things first.

Again. You're holding on to the man who doesn't love you. That causes you pain. You are only pained when you're doing what you don't want. What you really want is to be free of this pain. So when you say you know what you should do, you're really saying what you want: forget him. While you hold on to him no other man can come; you vibrate psychic waves of frustrated attachment. Who wants someone to love who's only half there because they love someone else? Do you think it only goes on in your head? Don't you realise yet after 48 years that you radiate energetically what you are and what you are not?

It wasn't up to you when you were born. It won't be up to you when you die. And it's not up to you to decide who is right for you and when you will meet him. If you could decide these things you probably wouldn't have married the man you did or be in the position you describe. Do what you want, not what you think you want. Be open to life, the new.

❖

Dear Barry

I am finding it very hard to resolve my last relationship. I met Jack on a retreat. Within a short time of our meeting he told me he 'loved me' and that I was his soul partner. He said that he had been told a long time before that he would meet me, that I had been described to him in detail and that I was exactly like the description. I didn't believe him. I thought he was crazy, though a 'nice guy'.

During the retreat we revealed our lives to each other. His was centred around his wife and lovely children — though he was unhappily married he said. Then we started to find we had great similarities in our lives. We shared all the same interests and had had all the same illnesses. Anyway, the days rolled on and we had to part. We both cried on our departure.

When I got home I contacted him and within two weeks he came to live with me. He told me that he knew he was being true to himself for the very first time. His wife went crazy and started ringing and coming round. She never let up in the five months we were together. The five months were utter bliss for both of us. He has since called it his 'grace' and that he was 'honoured' to have experienced such a relationship of giving on both sides.

But his children became ill and disturbed. They were a constant worry to Jack. He couldn't cope with it, so eventually he went back. We still met and sometimes made love. At times we experienced extraordinary feelings of rising up together and feelings of being in 'heaven' on earth. But after a few months he slowly sank back into normal married life.

Because of his feelings of dishonesty he stopped

coming to see me, though he still rang. Then that stopped. It was hell for me. He has told a mutual friend since that he still does and always will love me, that I am his soul partner and that we will continue our bliss together after death.

Now I am alone. I am trying very hard to practise what you say but I can't forget this extraordinary experience. I still cry from time to time, though I have to carry on.

But how do I get over this one? You have said 'It is passed'. But how can this be if we are to be together in the future? And how can I get a good relationship together knowing he is the other half of me?

With love to you from

Helen

Helen

No living man's body is your soul-mate. But man is your soul-mate. He is indeed in the flesh. But he is not in every body, nor does he have any particular man's body. He was in the flesh within the body of every man you have ever loved. He shone through them all, more or less. For this wonderful, beautiful man of yours is an energetic principle and he comes and goes in the flesh of the different bodies. It is always the same man, the same love, but in different men. He shone very strongly through Jack's body. But note, it was the flesh in the body called Jack, the indescribable feeling of oneness that you loved and recognised, not Jack's body. Your brain thought the body was the flesh — and so it misled you as it misleads everyone on earth.

You, too, are in the flesh; the woman of every man who

has ever loved you. You, too, are the flesh, not the body. And you shine forth to he who can see you until you or he start to lose the vision by perceiving the body and not the flesh. Then the love — or attraction — appears to fade.

In other words, the truth of love is in the flesh not in the body.

No two bodies can stay together for long. They're always on the move. The flesh is constant in every body, but the body is not. Men and women who perceive with the body fail to see the flesh for long and so the bodies must move on. Only the constant seeing of the flesh can keep two bodies staying together in love and truth. If one falters, they must part or be parted by distance or familiarity. Two bodies living together without flesh is the sham of love and our civilisation.

The similarities of the two bodies' lives as you describe is a partial reflection of the fact that you were to meet in the flesh — and then pass on.

For gone is Jack. And gone for him are you in the flesh. Let it be. You are still in the flesh to yourself — feel it? Feel your love? Wait and watch. He will come again in another body. Or you will meet in yours, eventually. But it won't be Jack. It will be your love, your own featureless, energetic man — he who never left you in the flesh, anyway, but only appeared to in the body.

❖

Dear Barry

Transcending self is a lonely time or so it seems. Since my heart was broken five years ago I have been learning steadily.

I feel or rather 'am' love constantly — this produces a peaceful life. Since I wrote to you three years ago I have moved from the sweet longing for love into its sweetness itself, an amazing feeling. This, though, has not been reflected, as yet, in events in my life. I have been endeavouring to find a job and have been told I am unemployable (I am over 45). Being a positive person I took whatever life turned up which was training as a counsellor. This, combined with what I know to be true, works well. Clients are not plentiful but life has always provided me with sufficient and always will.

I have transcended my 'emotional body' and have had incredible experiences of 'oneness'. My words cannot convey the completeness these experiences have bought me. All this seems contradictory to the next sentence. I 'know' where I am is right and time is unreal but I still feel unfulfilled as I need to share my love. Living in the now is essential to me as when my brain goes into future mode it could cause depression. As I have no job, no relationship and no social life I have plenty of hours in which to 'think and learn'. It is becoming increasingly difficult to avoid thinking. Is there anything else I can do besides living love in the now which will draw the loving feeling into an outer life?*

Love and light.

Leonora

* Emotional body: the unhappy entity in every body.

Leonora

All of us who would love God or life more at some time will reach a plateau where the only message is, 'Be still and know that I am God'. It is good and it is enough — but because our whole impetus is to love more, there is a quiet knowledge within that it is not sufficient, that fulfilment has not yet been filled. This is where you are.

You must wait. You know this. And I am only confirming what you know. Also, it will change. It may not change according to any expectations. But when it does — and I suspect it will happen soon — it will lead to a wider sense of sharing your love in existence. No one can say what this means. But write to me when it happens.

Meanwhile may I suggest that you open yourself like a good counsellor to life? You have much to give as you have seen through your professional counselling. This, what I am suggesting, must be a psychic opening — an opening whenever you walk down the street, in the bus, wherever you are, to the people, to the good of anyone in your silent being. If you can hear me rightly, this is giving without pre-conditioning. For we must truly give, or offer to all, to earn the right to share. (The use of your mature good sense will protect you from the clutching of those still too emotionally selfish to receive.) Be straight. Know what you don't want. But don't let what you don't like interfere.

❖

Barry

You are truly a champion of woman. Having experienced for many years the anguish, desolation, self-doubt, confusion and revulsion in the face of man's sexuality, it has been the most wonderful gift to hear you articulate so clearly the distinction between sex and making love: to confirm what I knew all along to be the truth. By speaking with such profundity and appreciation about woman, I feel seen and acknowledged for the first time. You are truly invoking the consciousness of woman, awakening the sleeping beauty. And you do so with such integrity and love, taking nothing for yourself. I am deeply grateful.

I would like to ask you about menopause. I am in my late 40's and see the process of physical disintegration occurring.

When I am in Me, I am connected with a timeless unchanging state and feel the beauty within. However, when I am focused on my physical reality and thoughts of the future, I have moments of insecurity and depression. When I was younger I used to console myself by thinking, 'Maybe I will be more beautiful next year'. Now I know there is no hope: it is all downhill from now on! I wonder if man will still be attracted to me as I get older. Will he still be able to love my body once it changes? There is a sense of trepidation about the physical and psychological changes I will go through in menopause.

Can you suggest how I can make a graceful transition through menopause into old age? What is the purpose of menopause?

With love and gratitude.

Megan

Megan

Menopause is the beginning of woman's transition from the gaining of experience of love into the wisdom and truth of love. Her once young, taut body begins to relax in the flesh as she sinks inside into a different place. This place is closer to Me, closer to the conscious state of the freedom of death. It is a transition lasting some years, which is fitting. In this time she actually undergoes what may be called a psychic rebirth. All the experience she has gathered, particularly of love and man is now to ripen, to mature. After the menopause she is supposed to be a more complete woman. All her cells will have been illumined by the value, the virtue, of her years to date. She is the living example of the young wine that having reached mid-age is now matured in wisdom and ready to give its enlightening nourishment.

I say 'supposed to be' because the graceful metre of this menopausal process has to a large extent been interrupted by our modern, competitive society and its negative influence on woman's natural knowledge of life and love. After the transition she is supposed to be the equivalent of the female guru, woman enlightened in the wonder and mysteries of love, wise in the ways of the world and particularly of man — the revered female teacher, example, or just plain mature woman. But today this is spoiled by her fears of getting old, her identification with her perceived body, her doubts regarding love, the comparison of herself with other women — all the negative judgements induced by the ignorant glossy magazine mentality.

Every woman undergoes the deeply maturing process in menopause. She does truly emerge from it a wiser and more loving, giving woman. But her mind often throws her into a mind-loop which prevents her from connecting with her newly illumined vital cells. She can seldom stop thinking and emotionalising, as your letter describes. Her mind, going round in circles, alienates her consciousness from the living love and wisdom stored in the cells. She is too busy competing, comparing and rueing what is past, too busy with her self — the common selfishness of our times — to be and enjoy the completion of the new vital body that has now been made.

All this of course is psychic or vital. It is psychic or vital — just as the cells of the body are psychic and vital — and not material as the mind thinks. The body is like a photograph in a newspaper. It's a good description of what has been but never a description of what is now. All that is vital, all that is life is in the cells now.

What you have to do first is hear the truth of what I am saying: sink gracefully into your cells and allow the menopausal rebirth to take your consciousness with it so that you may emerge a complete woman — good for any man to love, good for the younger generation and a contribution of value to the immortal vital body of mankind.

❖

The purpose of physical love is for the lovers to continually realise a greater love of God

❖

Dear Barry

I'm not quite sure how to begin this letter but perhaps I should start at the end and work back. My husband and I (married 15 years) listened to your 'Making Love' tapes and could feel the truth of them. We have both endeavoured to make love rightly but over the last month or so I have developed some sort of block and don't want him to enter me. I am not sure what this is about as we didn't ever have a problem with 'our sex life' or when we did eventually try to get our physical love right.

Perhaps I should now go to the beginning of the story. We met when we were both very young. I was very insecure. Here was a man I felt safe with; kind, loving, respectful. He felt like a long lost brother and whilst it wasn't or hasn't been an exciting relationship we agreed a lot on most things, although by nature I argue a lot. Still, we plodded on and always felt that there was more reason to stay together than there was to go our separate ways.

We have children now and I am involved very much in bringing them up but know that my husband must come first. We both badly want our marriage/love relationship to work but somehow there is something not right about it. The thought, though, of splitting up our home, our family and breaking away from the best friend I have in the world fills me full of heart-breaking emotion. I feel my heart is going to burst. I had the same feeling when I listened to your 'Songs of Life' tape when you sang about 'stand back'. I feel life is asking me to move away and I don't know if I can find the strength I need to show the kids. I know the emotion is not the truth of me but I am a very frightened child.*

It seems to me that I'm in a real Catch 22 situation here — not happy or alive in the relationship — but equally unhappy or even more unhappy about breaking away.

Even if I did break away, I would have to see my husband regularly and have our usual discussions about the kids/money etc (I've no way of supporting them or me at the moment). It would be a shame to break up unless it was absolutely necessary.

I hope, Barry, you can help me with the truth of this and show me the way. Thank you in anticipation.

Yours sincerely

Heather

PS It was about ten months ago when we first started trying to make love rightly. Perhaps I haven't given it enough time. Certainly, he thoroughly enjoys making love rightly (minus sex) but I have only enjoyed it on one occasion — the first time actually. On all other occasions, I've felt it goes on and on with no seeming end to it and it becomes more of an endurance test. Meantime I'm repeating to myself that I wish to offer this act up to a higher purpose.

Ironically whilst my body is not making love rightly with this man, it is the body that does not want to leave this house.

I know you will see through this shambles to the truth.

* 'Stand back': is one of the songs in the 'Songs of Life' tape and is an exhortation to stand back from the demands of the person, the emotional demands of the personal life.

Heather

You are in a dilemma which faces many married couples. You have closed off to your husband physically because he is no longer reaching you. You say, 'we didn't ever have a problem with our sex life' when you first listened to my 'Making Love' tapes. But the truth is you did, or one of you did, or you wouldn't have endeavoured, as you also say, to make love rightly. What happened was that in listening to the tapes you realised that something was missing in your love-life. And now you've subconsciously closed off, saying in your letter, 'I'm not sure what this is about'.

You talk about breaking away from your husband yet say it would be a shame to break up unless it was absolutely necessary.

Why then do you want to break up? You are bored with the love-making. Everything else is okay, you say, or would be okay. You need new energy. You need a man to love you with the vigour of passionately wanting you, which your husband is not doing. Isn't that the truth? That's what you're saying. But in our society, in the lie that most married couples live, this is not allowed to be said, let alone faced up to.

In our society such honesty usually means the end of the marriage. This is because the offended partner, due to his or her lack of love, is unable to face the truth of the situation that the energy between the two of them is exhausted; or because in making love to another there is always the possibility that the lover will discover a new world of love and not return.

Coming back to the partner will solve the situation in one way or another and show the reality of the love if any. The pair will break up or they will discover a new lease of life in their love and life together. Treating love personally by any of the people involved will cause even more emotion and unhappiness.

It is often easier for the man to continue in an exhausted situation. He is able to use his partner for orgasmic release — when he is allowed to or in circumstances where she dutifully submits or surrenders 'to a higher purpose' as you describe you are doing. She, as a rule, is not so orgasmically deft — unless clitorally abused* by him which, again, she will withdraw from as a finally unfulfilling substitute for love. Moreover, he is more likely than she to use fantasies to sustain his erstwhile passion. This dishonesty will also make her withdraw psychically or subconsciously since he will not be making love to her but to his fantasy.

Now the point of taking another lover in the above circumstances raises the crucial question of, what is the purpose of making love? Without this knowledge and the living of it, the making of love with another man will either end in the usual disaster and/or end in a repeat of the present dilemma — with perhaps the roles being reversed and the man being in your position.

To arrive at the correct answer so that you know what you are doing and are fit to take responsibility for love, you have to ask yourself these questions first. Are you fulfilling the purpose of making love with your husband as you have described it? If you take another lover will you again be fulfilling the purpose of making love; or will you lose yourself in excitement, the human love of change, or the confusion of not knowing what you're doing? It is because our society, and particularly the religions, are ignorant of any purpose to making love other than making babies, relieving sexual frustrations and anxieties, or simply having a good time, that love between man and woman has become such a tragic source of unhappiness.

The purpose of physical love is always for the lovers to descend into a greater realisation of the love of God. For you as woman this means to be continuously descending deeper into your own sweet mystery — which is the descent into the stillness and wonder of God or life within you. The power of this is then brought by you into your everyday life so that you realise an increasing harmony, fulfilment and authority in your external circumstances and in yourself. For man who truly loves or serves love it is the same. His loving energy takes you down and through your loving receiving of him, he descends into his own still and creative fullness. Each is then absorbed in the divine principle behind the symbolic union of man and woman's bodies joined in physical love. Then, as I say, that harmony is manifested in the world by always being true to love and simply living your life as the response to whatever has to be done without wanting, trying or anxious caring. Love directs your life.

You cannot realise this in a bored or boring partnership. And you can't do it by being promiscuous. It takes energy, the right energy of being true to love as love is and not as you would like to imagine it to be.

Anything less will not be in the spirit of what I am saying. And my words will be used by exploitative and manipulative sexual men and women for their own selfish ends and the perpetuation of unhappiness.

You say you hope I can help you with 'the truth of this' and show you the way. Well, is this the truth of it? Only you can say. And how can I show you the way? It is your life. I cannot live it for you and I cannot and will not tell you or anyone what to do. I can only tell you the truth as you ask for it, as I see it and know it.

But the final question is, is it the truth for you?

* Clitoral abuse: Barry Long teaches that man has taken the clitoris out of context in his love-making. By addicting woman to clitoral stimulation, man keeps woman focused on a more gross sensation rather than reaching her finer energies of love which reside in the deep recesses of the vagina.

Is your love not big enough to see the whole?

Dear Barry

About a year ago, Steve, whom I had been seeing occasionally since we had stopped working together, came to me in a loving way and we started seeing more of each other and had a (quiet) sexual relationship for a while. Then he went through a period of great insecurity and we continued to see each other but did not have a sexual relationship because in some way, it didn't seem right. However, for months we have been staying together in my flat quite often and had been getting on very well. It is not that I don't feel physically attracted to him or like to touch him, but when it comes to intercourse, it didn't feel right. In a way, I felt that it was sometimes hard enough to be with him because he was often quite emotional or something in some way I found difficult to handle. Then I decided to give up my job which I've done for many years and do some training. The same week that a replacement was found for me, Osho, as you know, died. This was a shock - though okay. Then Steve went off with another woman a couple of days later and I found this devastating. I have not come to terms with this and cannot understand why I feel like this about him and cannot be with him. He says he cares about me but is happy to be with this woman. I can understand that he wants a sexual relationship and he feels good with her.

That is the situation I am in. I am horrified sometimes because it seems as if suddenly many outside structures I have been living in have gone.

Thank you.

Carol

Carol

If you do not make love with the man you live with he will leave you for another woman. Or, he will become emotional, hard or edgy — tension will be there and sooner or later will erupt and shock you. You do not stay together with man to get on well. One, if not both of you, will be being dishonest.

So you were shocked, devastated as you say, when the inevitable happened. You thought it was all right — but it's never all right when you ignore the facts of life, that is, the facts of man and woman.

Then you were shocked again — of all things Osho died. Did you think he was going to live forever? You did. Again you thought it was all right — but it wasn't was it or you wouldn't have been shocked, even though it was okay.

You were right not to make love with Steve while it didn't feel right — as long as you confirmed the feeling in the act of making love. Otherwise it might be a case of the brain's favourite caper of disliking or living outside the action. That way it gets a feeling of experience or wilfulness — the power to decide things — without having to act.

Everything's never okay until you live without assumptions. That sort of alertness, or presence (of experience) eliminates living by likes and dislikes. It doesn't leave much — just the power to see things as they are, and not as you like to think they are.

You did not want him when you had him — and now he's gone to another woman you do. This is a brain caper. Its thoughts and pictures stir up the emotions and keep you distracted from the truth. This, the truth, you have stated in your letter.

You say you understand he wants a sexual relationship

(which you could not give him) and feels good with this woman. You have no problem with this. For in truth, Carol, your love is able to see this and accommodates it. That's the progress you have made in living the divine life. Your love and acceptance or understanding of the needs of love is greater, meaning more impersonal, than you think. The brain, the thinker, does not want you to be open and free like this. So it stirs the selfish emotions, the personal love, and you feel yourself divided.

You are the impersonal, Carol. Stay with it, be it: don't think back. Let him be where he is. He is too emotional, insecure for you. You know this.

To know, and finally to be, impersonal love is why you went to Rajneesh in the first place, or why you are with any master. You're just getting what you wanted, although the brain does not realise this. Here's the brain talking in the last sentence of your letter: 'I am horrified sometimes because it seems as if suddenly many outside structures I've been living in have gone'.

Precisely. You are being destructured, dismantled and detached — to be made worthy of impersonal love, which Thou are.

❖

Barry

My sister had a memory of my Dad sexually molesting her. We had a sense that something like this occurred but until now it was all vague enough for me to somewhat ignore. It was only confirmed yesterday but already I feel some new energy in myself — something has been released. At the same time there is anger and sadness. Barry, how do I forgive my father? My sister asked me this and all I could say was to stay with Me as much as she could, yet now, as the anger wells up inside I see how difficult it is to stay with Me.

Tears keep coming up. I try not to picture anything, not to get off on my imaginings, just to cry. This morning while I was meditating I wept, quiet calm tears. As the day goes on I feel the need to sob, to bring something up from deep in my chest. I don't find it so easy to sob without getting away from Me.

I just realised I forgot to mention that my Dad's been dead for many years. It feels as though that's all I have to say.

Anna

Anna

Did you love your father?

Since there is anger, sadness and sobbing you will find deep down that you did, or do, love him.

Even if you think you didn't love him, to be woman, real woman, you must face the fact of what love is, what it is to be love. You must out grow, rise above your selfish personal love which is your love of self.

Personal love is narrow and habitual. It imprisons a being in the past.

Is your love not big enough to see that your mother's lack of love, which you are perpetuating in asking me how to forgive your father, was the cause of his turning physically towards his daughter? Do you not see that your sister is not special — that she is just another victim of the lack of love that brings about a sort of madness on this planet? Do you not see, that you, in that little body there, as I in this little body here, am responsible for love? That while I cannot see life as it is, and the causes of events as they are, that I will blame yesterday's victims for today's victims? That I will be arrogant enough to think that I should forgive another for what they have done? That to have to forgive someone is to blame them, to suggest that you could never possibly do what they have done? Do you not see that such lack of love in yourself will raise a shadow between you and your partner or any other future partner you may have?

Everybody's a victim, not in the same way, for that is how we deceive ourselves of our selfish way of loving.

If you love your father the love of him is him, even though he is dead. Through the opening of your being within inform his love that you understand, that you hold nothing whatever against him, that you know he loved as best he could and that that is enough. Be joyous in this intimation. The love of your father will respond without form or information and you will know that love is — that love is real beyond death or birth.

You will then have put your father to rest — as well as that dead part of yourself.

Dear Barry

I have two questions to ask of you.

I am presently in a relationship with Sean which is fulfilling in many ways but I am puzzled at how remote and unattached we both feel when we are apart, as if we are not together as a couple — until we are back together physically — then it is like getting to know each other afresh each time and then moving into a calm, sometimes passionate, loving closeness when we make love. Then we part for the day, sometimes a night and we are like strangers again. This is not disturbing to me. But it seems as if we could walk away and it wouldn't matter. Sean says this is because we are both without emotion; but he also finds this unusual.

The other question is — I don't seem to dream or at least I don't remember my dreams. Why is this please?

With love from

Lorraine

Lorraine

The pain of the past (relationships) in you wants to suffer. It wants to miss Sean, to worry whether he's thinking about you etc, to feel the gratifying (to it) stimulation of being anxious, lonely (without him) — unhappy.

The woman that you are, the truly loving and loveable essence behind this dishonesty, is not disturbed at all by this 'strangeness' in your relationship. It simply enjoys the reality of man and woman being together in peace, passion, openness — the love that passes human understanding.

How wonderful is such love. You (and he) will not suffer when he dies or leaves you, as all things sooner or later must. Would you want your love to suffer? Human love, the love of pain you see embodied all around you, does. Human love — possessing, personalised love — makes people suffer and then has the audacity to say it doesn't want to or mean to.

The test (for your brain) is: do you enjoy being in each other's physical presence so that you are truly together when you are together? If the answer is 'Yes' — that's it. Enjoy yourselves. That is God's pleasure.

If you don't remember your dreams you don't need to. Remember God's in charge and love is.

❖

Only the
death of self
— the giving up of
wanting anything
but what is
— succeeds

❖

Dear Barry Long

Over the years I have meditated with different techniques. Sitting still: no problem, thoughts come and are dropped, but nothing happens.

Most days since I attended a seminar last year, I have listened to one or other of the tapes from the 'Myth of Life' series and 'How To Stop Thinking' — so returning to meditation.

Where is the incredible stillness and space, the joyful, the refreshing? Am I going to make a 'good' death if I am unable to consciously sink into that space?

Please don't get me wrong. I am a young, fit 71 year old female. I have joy and bliss (sometimes). I live alone and am full. I have no problems or worries, life is good.

The same care and attention I gave to giving birth (thrice) I want to give to dying when it comes. Please help me.

Pamela

Pamela

When you gave birth (thrice, as you say) you finally had to give up all questioning, all seeking, all choice, all personal willing. There was just what was happening, the mighty, irresistible process. There was nothing you could do but just surrender, be and witness, being.

Pain may have distracted you, but eventually attention even on that had to go. You were powerless perception.

So now, at 71 years, your long life, or labour, is supposed to have taught you to cease being distracted by your questioning, rationalising and choosing (what to do next) mind. For it was this mind that you finally disengaged from in childbirth — even down to its fears — as you faced the mighty continuous event of life as it is/was. There is no choice in life, only in the mind.

So please face now the same mightily continuous event of life. It's happening now. It's always happening now. No mind, no thought can describe it or understand it.

Do it. Be it. Then the incredible stillness and space, the joyful and the refreshing is.

Childbirth must have revealed this state to you, unless you obscured it with telling your mind's version of those events.

It was a matter of life and death then, I'll tell you. It's got to be a matter of life and death now, for the silly mind to give up. You've got to want it unto death. Then you will be the stillness of death while you are alive and you won't have to die rightly ever again because it is done.

Otherwise, do not be troubled. Sooner or later, when the moment of physical death arrives, you will again go through the choicelessness, the same mindless inevitability that is present in childbirth. Both are a matter of life and death and in that place the human mind collapses into stillness — there being nothing any longer worth thinking about.

Meditation cannot reach that place. It is merely a preparation, a slow-motion activity of the mind.

Only the death of self — the giving up of wanting anything but what is or what happens — succeeds.

Nonetheless, continue to do your best to be true to life, true to the situation and I will guarantee that in the moment of death you will sink into and be that place.

❖

BARRY LONG BOOKS AND TAPES MENTIONED IN THE TEXT

The Myth of Life is a series of seven tapes. It's a journey through the human psyche which forms our existence. Beginning with meditation, the series proceeds in self knowledge through the nature of truth, through the fact and truth of death, sexual love, right prayer, the world condition and the divine law or karma. Two tapes in this series mentioned in the text are 'Making Love' and 'May I Speak To You Of Death'.

Making Love is a two tape set teaching men and women to make love rightly, dealing with the source of sexual unhappiness; the true myth of love; emotionality and how to get rid of it; sexual problems and how to resolve them; the secrets of love-making; the way to find the passion and consciousness of making love divine.

May I speak to you of Death (referred to as the Death Tape) presents the fact of death without the fear. Barry Long describes what happens when you die; how to tell the children; how to cope with grief; the passage of death.

How to Stop Thinking This tape comprises ten lessons to help you stop thinking. Thinking is a disease of the human brain which leads to worry.

Songs of Life (referred to as the Songs Tape) is a tape of autobiographical songs which arose in Barry Long in his early 30's, when the one-pointed love of the divine 'pinned him inescapably, like a butterfly' and he left behind the life of an ordinary family man to become the master that he is now. He sings the songs and gives a commentary on each.

Talks from Tamborine Mountain were recorded monthly from Barry Long's home on Tamborine Mountain in Queensland, Australia from 1986 to 1990 and originally issued to regular subscribers. The tapes convey his reflections on living the life of the spirit in the everyday world. The Collected Talks are available and form a treasure of practical wisdom and inspirational teaching.

Journals Volumes One & Two

The Journal is the successor to the ***Talks from Tamborine Mountain***, a daily record of Barry's realisation and penetrating observations of the truth behind the changing world of events and circumstances.

Stillness is the Way

An Intensive Meditation Course

This book is a record of three days of teaching by Barry Long. It follows the process experienced by several people as he teaches them over the course of a weekend, steadily going deeper into meditation and undoing the resistance of the mind.

Only Fear Dies

A Book of Liberation

Formerly published as *Ridding Yourself of Unhappiness,* this book is a clear and challenging account of the way problems are created in ourselves and in society and how you can eliminate them from your life and return to a more natural and effortless way of living.

For a complete catalogue of Barry Long publications write to one of the contact addresses at the end of this book.

❖

SUBJECT GUIDE

CURRENT INTERNATIONAL CONTACT ADDRESSES (1994)

AUSTRALIA
PO Box 5277, Gold Coast MC, Qld 4217
Tel 075 767665 Fax 075 767641

ENGLAND
42 North Street, Wiveliscombe, Somerset, TA4 2LA
Tel 01984 623426 Fax 01984 624446

FINLAND
c/o Neitsytsaarentie 9b C72, 00960 Helsinki
Tel 0 341 3063

GERMANY
c/o Krochmannstrasse 2A, 22299 Hamburg
Tel 040 511 7870

HOLLAND
c/o ZaZen, Zoutmanstraat 16A, 2518 GP Den Haag
Tel 070 365 9016 Fax 070 345 7447

SWEDEN
c/o Box 4311, 102 67 Stockholm
Tel 08 644 3004

USA
c/o PO Box 251, Cerrillos, New Mexico, NM 87010
Tel/Fax 505 474 4830

The latest publications catalogue, mailorder details and seminar booking information can always be obtained via

The Barry Long Foundation
BCM Box 876, London WC1N 3XX, England